ENDORSE

Radical Healing is unique among many books on my shelves that deal with the subject of healing. Ben brilliantly shows that wholeness must start from inside one's heart, and then it must be allowed to work its way outward to bring healing and wholeness into every realm of a person's life. I especially love that each chapter ends with a summary and a suggestion about how to activate what has been read. In this book, Ben will importantly show you the path to healing—how to uproot and demolish what is wrong in your soul and how to move forward into wholeness. Then he provides an encouraging test to reveal whether you have attained the wholeness you need. This is a superior book because it starts at the heart level, which is where healing must begin if it is to be sustained over time. In addition to endorsing this book, I want to encourage you to read it from beginning to end. As a result, you'll not only be bettered as an individual, you'll be more equipped to help others you encounter in life who are in need of healing and wholeness.

Rick Renner
Minister, Author, Broadcaster
Moscow, Russia

The current total of your experiences has largely shaped your life. This includes the positives and the negatives, starting with the environment you were raised in. Without a revelatory understanding of the Word of God, much of what impacts us goes back to family complexities, social memories, and where we sense that we fit into today's rapidly changing culture.

Additionally, when considering the future, there is a silent anxiety that many seem to stuff and accumulate. Even more are those who have been affected by health issues, the loss of a loved one, or the navigation of betrayal and regret. With certainty, a vigilant response is required to deal with all of life's tapestry. An aggressive counter to so much of the emotional debt and crisis fatigue so many are bearing to the point of near collapse. This is the cause of deep sadness and issues that manifest in so many. They could never find reprieve or any answers to the fight inside.

After reading Ben Díaz's book *Radical Healing*, I realized just how important it is to address these internal issues. Ben deals with these things like a surgeon, identifying the problem, then prescribing what must be done, and finally offering the equivalent of scheduling the necessary procedure. This book will help you answer the fight inside by providing real solutions and hope!

Something that must be said is that my friend Pastor Ben is not talking from a theoretical point of view—instead, this man has lived out the concepts of what he is offering in the pages ahead. My wife Heather and I watched and prayed as he and his family walked through tremendous adversity that seemed to come on them suddenly from every direction. To my delight, I watched him stand up and apply what he offers you in this book. Pastor Ben Díaz earned my deepest respect as a father and husband and a man of impeccable integrity. When battles came, Ben did not collapse. Rather, he rose to meet them, and as the pressure in its various forms so often does—it reveals what is inside a person. What was revealed in my friend was the mark of a true man of God who lives what he preaches. It is my honor to endorse and recommend this book to everyone wholeheartedly. I know the man who wrote it, and you will benefit from his wisdom and the excellent principles he has laid out, which are waiting to be discovered by you!

Excellent work, Ben! Your life speaks so loudly to what you teach that I just had to read this book!

Joseph Z
Author, Broadcaster, Prophetic Voice
JosephZ.Com

I've witnessed firsthand the transformative power of Pastor Ben Díaz's ministry. Visiting his church, I saw hundreds of lives changed forever through his unique blend of Spirit-led teaching and biblical psychology. Ben's groundbreaking approach has been distilled into this accessible, life-changing book *Radical Healing*. Get ready for a miracle in your life as you apply the principles and insights within these pages.

Lance Wallnau
Author of *God's Chaos Candidate*, *God's Chaos Code*, and *7 Mountain Mandate*
CEO of Lance Learning Group
Founder of Lance Wallnau Ministries

In *Radical Healing*, you are holding a blueprint for breakthrough in your hands! In Matthew 11:19 (NLT), Jesus says, "Wisdom is shown to be right by its results." I have known Pastor Ben for several years and can testify to the fact that he has lived out the principles outlined in this book as evidenced by the freedom, fruit, and favor in his life. If you are eager to grab ahold of all the promises God has for you, this is a must-read!

Billy Epperhart
CEO of Andrew Wommack Ministries and Charis Bible College
Founder of Wealth Builders International

Radical Healing: Winning the Battle for Your Mind, Will, and Emotions is a hope-filled book that brings healing to those who have experienced disappointment, but it also releases grace for victory and wholehearted living. Ben Díaz has overcome much in his own life and has helped many find freedom and peace in difficult times. Throughout this book, you will receive wisdom, insight, and an impartation on how you too can heal your life and increase your influence. Each chapter is filled with real-life testimonies of how healing, prayer, and declarations set us up for the breakthrough we are contending for. This is a needed book in this hour.

Steve Backlund
Co-founder of Igniting Hope Ministries
Bethel Leaders Network Leadership and BSSM Instructor

Radical Healing is a must-read for anyone not walking in the fullness of the abundant life Jesus promised us. This well-written book is loaded with not only great teaching and profound insights, but also many practical and useful everyday exercises that you can follow right away. I'm convinced this book is going to bring great breakthrough in your life, especially in the areas you've been seemingly stuck in.

I've had the honor and pleasure of knowing Pastor Ben, not only as a co-laborer and ministry associate, but also as a close personal friend. I can recommend him, and this book—his first, hopefully of many!—wholeheartedly, without any hesitation. I've watched him lead his vibrant church, his delightful family, and himself with humility, integrity, and wisdom beyond his years.

I urge you to devour this book and let the Lord heal your heart through its principles!

Ashley Terradez
President and Founder of Terradez Ministries and Global Church Family

The world is in chaos, battered by the winds of anxiety, lies, and shame, and needs voices that are equipped to lead God's people beside still waters and green pastures to restore their souls. Ben Díaz is one of those voices—a gift to the body of Christ. His book *Radical Healing* is a road map for breakthrough and wholeness.

Tom Crandall
Overseer of Evangelism at Bethel Church Redding, California
Founder, 1hope4America

Are you ready to break free from frustration and disappointment? *Radical Healing* is your road map to freedom, wholeness, and walking in God's promises. Pastor Díaz doesn't peddle another spiritual formula or quick fix. Instead, he reveals a biblical process that heals the broken places of the heart and renews the mind to align fully with Christ. If you're tired of going in circles and longing for real, lasting breakthrough, this book is your answer. It's time to step into the wholeness God designed for you!

Alan DiDio
Pastor of The Encounter Charlotte
and Host of *Encounter Today*

I have had the privilege of ministering in Vida Church and getting to know Ben and his beautiful wife and children. Ben is a tremendous example of one who has passion for the things of God and for his call as a pastor. *Radical Healing* is an anointed book that dives deep into the true nature of the heart and God's provision for healing on every level of life. I highly recommend this revelatory teaching and know that it will bless you!

Barry Bennett
Senior Instructor at Charis Bible College
Woodland Park, Colorado

Pastor Ben and Kara Díaz are amazing pastors with a great heart for people and seeing them walk in the revelation of God's Word that brings victory. In his new book, *Radical Healing*, Pastor Ben shows us the way to victorious Christian living through identifying the source of our problems and our victory: "our heart condition." This new book will help you get a grip on life and begin to walk in God's promises at brand-new levels.

Pastor Lawson Perdue
Charis Christian Center
Colorado Springs, Colorado

We couldn't be more thrilled to endorse our dear friend Ben's book, *Radical Healing*. We've had the joy of knowing Ben and Kara for over 15 years, and in that time, we've seen them live out an extraordinary faith—one that breaks past the usual boundaries and brings deep, lasting change. This book is a powerful extension of who they are: it's about finding freedom from toxic cycles, stepping into God's promises, and aligning with His heart for wholeness. Ben doesn't just talk about faith; he lives it in a way that's contagious, bringing hope and transformation to everyone around him. We've watched him face life's challenges with incredible grace, and we've seen the undeniable impact of God's love in his life and his family. If you're looking to experience real healing and walk in the fullness of what God has for you, this book will be a true gift. We highly recommend it!

Bob and Audrey Meisner
Bestselling Authors, *Marriage Under Cover*
Podcasters, All About Relationships
bobandaudrey.com

I want to recommend this book to you, *Radical Healing*, written by my good friend, Pastor Ben Díaz. This is a must-read for anyone who is struggling with chronic physical symptoms or negative behavioral patterns and has not experienced the freedom Jesus paid for at the cross. In this book, Ben shares from personal revelation and experience the process of identifying the root issues of the heart that are the cause of many problems so many in the church are dealing with. I love the chapter summaries and practical activation steps he provides at the end of each chapter. Ben is a great man of integrity, man of the Word, husband, father, pastor, and teacher. I am confident you will be equipped to walk in greater freedom and help others with their heart issues through the principles shared in this book.

Greg Mohr
Founder of Greg Mohr Ministries
Director of Ministry School and Staff Instructor at Charis Bible College

Radical Healing is not just a book—it's a divine tool for transformation. Pastor Ben Díaz writes with piercing clarity about the importance of addressing the pain in our hearts and allowing the Holy Spirit to bring healing. This book is a road map for every believer who longs to live from a place of wholeness rather than manage symptoms or avoid pain.

As someone who has experienced the effects of unresolved pain, I can testify to the truth of this message. In 2020, I lost two family members to overdoses. Instead of mourning, I busied myself with ministry and outreach. But in 2021, a mentor lovingly confronted me, pointing out how my avoidance of pain was affecting my heart and my ability to lead. It wasn't until I surrendered to God's healing process that I experienced freedom. This book reminds us that transformation begins with the heart, not by ignoring the pain but by letting the Holy Spirit address it at its root.

Ben's powerful analogy of pain being like a "check engine light" resonates deeply. Ignoring it only leads to greater issues—just as mold from an undetected leak spreads and causes destruction. The call to stop trimming weeds and address the root of the problem is a wake-up call for every believer. Pastor Ben equips readers with practical tools like reflective questions, biblical insights, and Spirit-led steps to address the wounds of the soul.

Radical Healing is a must-read for anyone who desires to be made whole and live in the abundant life Jesus offers. Whether you are a leader, a minister, or simply a believer seeking healing, this book will guide you to a place of deep restoration and freedom. Let this book be the companion that takes you into the heart of God for your life. I wholeheartedly recommend it to everyone.

Chris Overstreet
Evangelist and Founder of Compassion to Action

Both powerful and transparent! Ben takes readers on a transformative journey through personal experiences, scriptural insights, and powerful revelations on faith. After witnessing God's miraculous work in healing and restoration, a life-altering motorcycle accident challenges his long-held beliefs about faith and healing. This pivotal moment ignites a quest for deeper understanding, leading to the discovery of a crucial piece missing from traditional teachings.

The book provides readers with practical tools—prayer, meditation, and declaration—to uproot negative beliefs and embrace the fullness of God's promises. The author's candid storytelling, combined with biblical wisdom, invites readers to engage sincerely with their faith, confront past traumas, and cultivate a heart aligned with God's truth.

If you're yearning for breakthrough, healing, and a richer understanding of God's promises, this book is a must-read. It will inspire you to open your heart and embark on your own journey toward wholeness and renewed faith.

Carlie Terradez
Co-Founder of Terradez Ministries

As tripartite creatures, it is important for us, as children of God, to understand how each part of our makeup works. It's imperative we understand that we are spirits that have souls that exist in bodies. We need to grasp that God, in His Word, deals with our spirits, and when we take what His Word is speaking to our spirits and act on it, it positively affects our flesh. It also causes us to be spiritually minded, which influences our souls in the right way.

In my humble opinion, Pastor Ben Díaz adequately addresses the part of us that finds itself in the middle of a battle between our born-again spirits and our unregenerate flesh: our souls. The internal wounds, the scars of the heart, the guilt and shame that attempt to permanently take up residence in our lives are all found in the soul. This is an excellent book that helps the believer keep their mind renewed according to the Word. I highly recommend this book with its user-friendly reading and practical application that is sure to bring about change in our lives and healing to our souls.

Dr. Fred Price Jr.
Senior Pastor of Crenshaw Christian Center

Radical
HEALING

FOREWORD BY TROY BREWER

Radical HEALING

WINNING THE BATTLE FOR
YOUR MIND, WILL
& EMOTIONS

BEN DÍAZ

© Copyright 2025– Ben Díaz

Printed in the United States of America. All rights reserved. No portion of this book may be reproduced, stored in a retrieval system, or transmitted in any form or by any means—electronic, mechanical, photocopy, recording, scanning, or other—except for brief quotations in critical reviews or articles, without the prior written permission of the publisher. Unless otherwise identified, Scripture quotations are taken from the Holy Bible, New Living Translation, copyright 1996, 2004, 2015. Used by permission of Tyndale House Publishers, Wheaton, Illinois 60189. All rights reserved.

Scripture quotations marked NIV are taken from the HOLY BIBLE, NEW INTERNATIONAL VERSION®, Copyright © 1973, 1978, 1984, 2011 International Bible Society. Used by permission of Zondervan. All rights reserved.

Scripture quotations marked NKJV are taken from the New King James Version. Copyright © 1982 by Thomas Nelson, Inc. Used by permission. All rights reserved.

Scripture quotations marked KJV are taken from the King James Version.

Scripture quotations marked TPT are taken from *The Passion Translation*, Copyright © 2017, 2018, 2020 by Passion & Fire Ministries, Inc., www.thepassiontranslation.com. Used by permission of BroadStreet Publishing Group, LLC, Racine, Wisconsin, USA. All rights reserved.

Scripture quotations marked ESV are taken from The Holy Bible, English Standard Version® (ESV®), copyright © 2001 by Crossway, a publishing ministry of Good News Publishers. Used by permission. All rights reserved.

Scripture quotations marked NASB are taken from the NEW AMERICAN STANDARD BIBLE®, Copyright © 1960, 1962, 1963, 1968, 1971, 1972, 1973, 1975, 1977, 1995, 2020 by The Lockman Foundation. Used by permission.

Scripture quotations marked AMPC are taken from the Amplified® Bible, Classic Edition, Copyright © 1954, 1958, 1962, 1964, 1965, 1987 by The Lockman Foundation. All rights reserved. Used by permission.

All emphasis within Scripture quotations is the author's own.

Published by Harrison House Publishers
Shippensburg, PA 17257

ISBN 13 TP: 978-1-6675-0939-6
ISBN 13 eBook: 978-1-6675-0940-2

For Worldwide Distribution, Printed in the U.S.A.
1 2 3 4 5 6 7 8 / 29 28 27 26 25

I dedicate this book to my dad, Benjamin Díaz Valasis, the best dad in the world. You went to heaven too soon. Thank you for truly making your ceiling my floor. You really set me up for success, Dad. I love you.

ACKNOWLEDGMENTS

To my Lord and King Jesus, to my Perfect Father in heaven, and to the precious Holy Spirit, thank You. Everything good in my life comes from You. You're my everything, and my life is forever Yours and for Your purposes. Thank You for trusting me with influence, resources, and revelation to make You famous and to bring heaven on earth.

To my wife, Kara—you make me better in every way, and you made this book better in so many ways. Thank you for believing in me and helping me finish this book.

Thank you, Hannah Grieser, for your writing gift and skills that made this book possible.

Thank you, Makenzie Skinner, for your incredible editing gift and for gifting your precious time to this project.

Thank you, Kyle Loffelmacher, for believing in me and the message God gave me in this book.

CONTENTS

Foreword		xiv
Introduction: When You Know What to Do but It Isn't Working		1
1	It All Boils Down to One Thing	4
2	Doing the ~~Hard~~ Heart Work	18
3	The Worst Day of My Life	27
4	A Different Kind of Battle	41
5	Praying to Uproot	51
6	Meditating to Plant	67
7	Declaring to Build	84
8	A Biblical Prayer for Wholehearted Healing	100
9	The Evidence of a Healed Heart	113
Epilogue: One of My Supernatural Testimonies		123
About Ben Díaz		127

FOREWORD

In the journey of life, there are pivotal moments that redefine our path, sculpting us into vessels capable of weathering the fiercest storms, and it is in these moments that we discover our true identity, not just as creations but as co-creators with Christ in the masterpiece that is our life.

When Ben approached me about his idea for a book on healing the heart, God moved my spirit and I willingly sowed into this book because people of faith need to hear this amazing message he has for us. *Radical Healing: Winning the Battle for Your Mind, Will, and Emotions* by Benjamin Díaz is a testament to this divine partnership—a guide that beckons us into the depths of our hearts, urging us to confront and heal the wounds that hinder our walk with God.

As I perused the chapters of Ben's work, I was struck by the profound simplicity and the radical call to arms against the unseen forces that battle for our hearts. This book is not merely a manual for self-improvement; it is a divine invitation to engage in the heart work necessary for genuine transformation. Man, I love that! The example of the Leaning Tower of Pisa gives a great visual on the foundation of a vulnerable heart. Benjamin Díaz points out because the foundation was clay, the tower had no chance of withstanding any more pressure and weight. In the book there is a phrase that is really a divine revelation. The phrase, "if we don't heal our hearts, the enemy will continue to attack us at our most vulnerable areas" is such a true statement and it is reflected in the story of the Leaning Tower of Pisa, which was vulnerable at its foundation.

Through the lens of biblical wisdom and personal revelation, Díaz navigates the complex terrains of healing, prayer, and the power of the Word, equipping believers to reclaim their identity and purpose in

Christ. At the core of this transformative journey is the understanding that our hearts are the battlegrounds on which our destinies are forged. As Proverbs 4:23 (NIV) admonishes, "Above all else, guard your heart, for everything you do flows from it." Díaz masterfully unpacks this truth, challenging readers to delve into the heart of their struggles, confronting the lies, fears, and strongholds that have kept them in bondage.

In a world increasingly marked by superficiality and evasion, this call to authenticity and deep healing is both countercultural and desperately needed. Prayer, meditation, and declaration are presented not as religious rituals but as dynamic, life-giving practices that help intimate encounters with the living God. These spiritual disciplines become the tools through which we excavate the depths of our hearts, uprooting the weeds of the past and planting the seeds of God's truth. Díaz's personal anecdotes and scriptural insights illuminate the path to healing, reminding us that while the journey may be fraught with challenges, it is also replete with the promise of God's faithful presence and transformative power. As a fellow traveler on this journey of faith, I am deeply moved by the vulnerability and wisdom encapsulated in these pages.

Radical Healing resonates with the heartbeat of the gospel—a message of redemption, restoration, and relentless love. Benjamin Díaz has extended an invitation to embark on a pilgrimage of the heart, one that promises to lead us into the fullness of life Christ has ordained for us. To those who find themselves weary from the battles, to the brokenhearted, and to anyone yearning for a deeper, more authentic relationship with God, this book is a beacon of hope. It is a reminder that healing is not only possible but is part of our inheritance as children of God. As you engage with the truths presented in this book, may you experience the profound peace, joy, and freedom that come from being wholeheartedly healed by the Great Physician. The journey of healing is not a solitary endeavor but a communal voyage, a testament to the power of shared stories and collective faith. As you delve into the pages of *Radical Healing*, know that you are not alone. Together, let us embrace the heart work, stepping boldly into the promise of Jeremiah 30:17 (NIV), "'But I will restore you to health and heal your wounds,' declares the Lord."

In Christ,
Troy Brewer
Senior Pastor of Open Door Church in Burleson, Texas
Author of *31 Battle Cry Declarations, Redeeming Your Timeline, Numbers That Preach, Good Overcomes Evil, Looking Up,* and *Soul Invasion*
TroyBrewer.com ODX.tv

INTRODUCTION

WHEN YOU KNOW WHAT TO DO BUT IT ISN'T WORKING

I grew up in a wonderful Baptist home in Mexico City, but I first encountered the Holy Spirit at age 13. From that moment, God took me on a journey of experiencing the supernatural and seeing miracles at a young age. At 17, I laid hands on the blind, the deaf, and people with all kinds of sickness and disease, and I saw God heal them instantly. At 18, I joined a missionary team and organized miracle crusades all over Mexico and Central America. I saw the undeniable power of God at work in miraculous ways in the forms of healings, provisions, restorations, divine appointments, favor, protection, and so much more. I learned that faith works, God's promises are true, and the power of God is for us today.

Well, it works until it doesn't...

In April 2021, I broke myself. I've never needed a miracle per se, but I've lived by God's promises since I was 13. There's a difference between needing an emergency miracle and living by faith in God's Word—seeing it manifested in your life day after day. I had only done the latter up until that day.

That Saturday morning in April, I had a near-death experience. I was in a motorcycle accident deep in the desert. As I was lying in the hospital that night after realizing I wasn't going to walk out of there without a cast and that this was possibly the beginning of a long recovery journey, I remember thinking, *What went wrong? I declared the name of Jesus. I truly expected to walk out that day. I prayed in tongues. So why didn't it work?*

The Bible tells us that hope deferred makes the heart sick (Proverbs 13:12). Maybe this is you. Maybe you've believed, confessed, prayed, and sowed, but your heart feels sick because you see the people next to you getting the promises manifested in their lives but it doesn't seem to be happening for you. Maybe you've even seen people who have been saved for only minutes receive supernatural answers to prayers that you yourself have been praying for decades.

In this book, I will share with you a huge truth I was missing, and it's *not more faith!* I realized that what I was missing had never been taught in any of the churches I'd attended. This missing piece has transformed my life, my family, and my church congregation. I will share my journey, my experiences, and the breakthrough that came through this one revelation the Holy Spirit gave me during one of the hardest seasons of my life. I believe this revelation can change your life forever like it did mine, and it will unlock many promises you've been standing on for too long.

Have you ever asked:

- Is God really good?
- Why does this keep happening to me?
- Is there something wrong with me?
- Are God's promises and His power really for everyone?
- Is the problem that I don't have enough faith, or that I don't pray enough, read the Bible enough, serve enough, or give enough?
- Are His promises only for a few special ministers?
- Does God care about this part of my life?

Well, let me tell you that the truth the Holy Spirit revealed to me will set you free on a whole new level and will ignite your faith in places where disappointment has quenched your desire to believe God's rich promises for too long.

The best part? It is so much simpler than you can imagine.

You already have what it takes for your breakthrough. You won't need to attend another conference or get prayed for by a special person or buy anything. All you need is to open your heart to receive the same understanding and revelation that God gave me through His Word in this life-changing journey.

CHAPTER 1

IT ALL BOILS DOWN TO ONE THING

I have the best job in the world! I take care of people from birth to death.

That's right. I've been a pastor since 2008. During that time, I have seen many ups and downs for my congregation, but there's nothing more disheartening than watching people who love God and attend church week after week fall into the same problems time and time again. I'm telling you, I've witnessed well-intended people trying so hard not to fall into the same destructive patters over and over—so they don't get into a financial mess again, so their marriages improve, or their homes remains in peace. Sometimes the change seems to last for a little while but they end up in that same ditch again.

I have also seen many people break free from those destructive cycles and never fall back into them again. Many of whom are still in our church today, and they are a reminder to me that God's way to freedom works, that heart transformation will always trump behavior modification.

I tell people all the time, behavior modification happens when all you have is "religion" (a bunch of dos and don'ts) but no relationship with the Holy Spirit. It is like wearing makeup—it only lasts a day and then you need to reapply. Of course, I only know this from watching my wife, but even a clown could not keep his makeup on permanently. It would start melting, distorting, and looking creepy. And that's how religious people look—fake, like something isn't adding up. The outside is starting to tell a different story about the inside.

It All Boils Down to One Thing

On the other hand, heart transformation is permanent, and once it happens, it adjusts the behavior effortlessly to match the inside. Religion forces you to match your outside to a book of rules you have no relationship with.

This is where many Christians find themselves—stuck in the same destructive cycles, negative mindsets, and harmful addictions. We know so many promises of God, but we can't seem to get them to manifest. And if this is you, it's likely not due to a lack of trying. In fact, you may have tried praying. You tried reading your Bible. You tried the church services, retreats, and consumed the Christian content and courses. However, nothing seems to be working, and you still feel broken. I can hear your cry because it was once my cry. I longed to experience the promises I read about in the Bible and see fruitfulness in areas that had been barren for far too long. Many times, I even struggled to rejoice in the testimonies of others because I would wonder, *But what about me?*

Well, God answered my cry and gave me a revelatory, simple strategy for healing and experiencing breakthrough in all those areas of frustration in our lives. That's what this book is about, and I have good news: It's easier than you think!

It all boils down to one thing—the heart. The heart is the control center of our lives. So as we embark on this healing journey to become whole, we will learn how to co-labor with the Holy Spirit to heal the places of brokenness in our hearts that are affecting these different areas of our lives.

Before you think this is too simple or you don't need this "heart stuff" because you're a new creation, let me propose to you that this might be the very reason you're not experiencing life and life more abundant in every aspect of your life. Jesus said in John 10:10 (NIV), "I have come that they might have life and life more abundant." So if we're new creations, why aren't we experiencing it? It is because we still need to be transformed by renewing our minds. This has to do with our belief systems, the beliefs of our hearts that we're not even aware of. Those are the ones affecting you more than the ones you're aware of.

Song of Songs 2:15 talks about the little foxes that go underground, where they can't be seen, and spoil the vines, eating the roots of the harvest and destroying it. It is the same with our heart beliefs.

Let me show you.

Proverbs 4:23 says, "Guard your heart above all else, for it determines the course of your life." The New King James Version puts it like this: "Keep your heart with all diligence, for out of it spring the issues of life."

Your heart beliefs will determine your life's trajectory and every issue you encounter along the journey. The state of your relationships, finances, family, health, career, and emotional well-being all flow from your heart. All the issues of life flow from the heart, whether good or bad. We're not talking about head knowledge, which is why we can know the Word of God, know the right answers, know the right methods, and still produce something completely different. You can share what you know, but you will reproduce what you truly believe.

In the opening words of his book *Renovation of the Heart*, renowned theologian Dallas Willard writes, "We live from our hearts. The part of us that drives and organizes our lives is not the physical." On a scientific level, this could not be more true. The heart drives and organizes every system in the body by pumping life-giving blood to every one of our cells. If a harmful toxin enters the heart or the heart experiences too much pressure, everything else in the body is negatively affected. Yet the heart is so much more than a red, throbbing, fist-sized blob in our bodies. It represents what we desire, what we love, and the choices we make.

When the Old Testament was written, humans had no concept of the brain. They did not even have a word for it! Instead, they thought the heart was the source of all intellectual activity. So, the Hebrew word for *heart* (*lēb̠*) was used in various ways. In the Bible, *lēb̠* describes the inner man, mind, will, heart, understanding, seat of appetites, emotions, passions, and courage, to name a few (Strong's H3820). In other words, the heart is the source of everything. Did you know that around 80 percent of a child's belief system is written in his or her heart by the age of eight? Life experiences are constantly writing things in our hearts. We are always learning and renewing our minds to something. Children create most of their beliefs in their home. Parents and experiences only solidify those lessons. They then become part of our subconscious telling us what, how, and why to expect things, and as we see experiences show up in our lives repeatedly they become stronger beliefs, whether good or bad.

Jesus Came for the Brokenhearted

In Luke 4:18 (NKJV), Jesus says, "The Spirit of the Lord is upon Me, because He has anointed Me to preach the gospel to the poor; He has sent Me to heal the brokenhearted, to proclaim liberty to the captives and recovery of sight to the blind, to set at liberty those who are oppressed."

Every human will experience a broken heart at some point in his or her life. Pain and disappointment are inevitable parts of the human experience. Jesus warned, "Here on earth you will have many trials and sorrows. But take heart, because I have overcome the world" (John 16:33). How you take it to heart will determine its effect on you. The meaning you assign to experiences will determine the story you write on your heart. Let me give you an example of something that happened to me.

When I first got married, my wife Kara would greet me at the door with a hug and a kiss when I got home from work. I loved this. It filled up my love tank and made me feel like a million dollars! A few years into marriage, I noticed she stopped meeting me at the door. I started subconsciously adding meaning to it, and that meaning wasn't good. I was writing a story in my mind, daily meditating on it, and gathering evidence. The fact that she wasn't coming to the door to receive me like before proved to me she was not in love with me and she wasn't attracted to me anymore. It made me feel unloved and rejected. You see, pain isn't always truth but it's real. The truth, however, was very different than the meanings and stories I had chosen to believe. These meanings were causing me pain and were also affecting my marriage because of my self-inflicted feelings of rejection. The truth was that we had started having children. We had baby after baby—five of them for eight years. My amazing wife, who passionately loved me even more than the day we got married, was a little busy during those moments I would come home from work. She was cooking, feeding kids, making kids do their homework, cleaning up messes, and sometimes getting ready to counsel someone later that night. Her not coming to the door to greet me with a hug and a kiss after my comparatively breezy day at work had nothing to do with her love for me.

The meaning we assign to our experiences can create room for fear, lies, and debilitating beliefs. Depending on how we cope with or numb the pain, we can often create cycles of addiction, too. So, how we react to, process, and heal from pain and disappointment is vital.

Proverbs 13:12 clues us into the negative effects disappointment can have on our hearts. It says, "Hope deferred makes the heart sick, but a dream fulfilled is a tree of life."

People are hurting, and Jesus came to heal the brokenhearted. Christians, even those who walk closely with God, are not exempt from this condition. However, what you do between deferred hope and the fulfilled dream is critical. The remedy for wounded hearts is to invite God's healing into the brokenness and trust Him until He restores your pain into a tree of life. It is very important you stay with me throughout this book because I'm going to teach you a powerful tool that will walk you through healing your heart with God in a very practical way. But it will only work if you have the understanding. Many people just want the recipe, the formula, or the right prayer; but without the understanding we are establishing here, these will only leave you with a religious practice and no real transformation.

As a pastor, I see people ignore their pain and continue with life as though nothing has happened. Pain is like the check engine light in our cars. The check engine light indicates that we need to fix something. Pain is alerting us to something going on in our hearts that is hurting us. But instead of slowing down, many of us ignore the warning signs of pain and repeated toxic cycles and continue in life as usual. People in ministry who are hurting keep building their ministries, discipling others, and pouring into their families—all good things. But when they get quiet, they still feel broken inside. They wonder why the Word of God is not working in their lives like it is for other believers. Consequently, trust issues bubble underneath the surface.

There is nothing more frustrating than knowing truth—The Word of God—but not seeing it manifest in your life. It's a heart issue not an "I need more faith" issue.

A Heart Divided

Every issue in your life right now is flowing from your heart's beliefs. We can have head knowledge and heart beliefs contradicting each other without even realizing it. Our hearts can be divided, and as Jesus said, "Every city or house divided against itself will not stand" (Matthew 12:25 NKJV). Dallas Willard compared the human heart to the CEO of a major company. Just because a CEO makes a decision does not always mean it will be executed, nor will everyone in the company be on the same page. Our heart can also be confusing because it is more connected with the subconscious beliefs we're unaware of. When our heart has a contrary belief to that of our head we call it cognitive dissonance. It is like having an internal civil war, a double personality, an internal division, or as Paul put it in Romans 7:15 (NIV), "I do not understand what I do. For what I want to do I do not do, but what I hate I do." (We will expand on this concept further in a later chapter.)

I love doing puzzles, taking a bunch of scattered pieces and putting them together to create a beautiful picture. The beginning stages of a puzzle are always confusing. The pieces are sprawled out in a chaotic mess on the table, and there is little semblance of the final product. However, thanks to the box cover, you know what final picture you are aiming for. If you are like me, this disconnect can be frustrating. I know what the picture should look like, but I can't seem to get there. This is precisely how many of us feel when we read the Bible but don't see God's promises come to pass. As Christians, we can have a lot of the answers to the problems we face, but we don't always know how to put the pieces together. We envision a pretty picture of what our lives could look like, but in reality, we are dealing with a bunch of scattered pieces.

Applying the Word of God to our lives is how we put the pieces together. Knowing it is not enough. In other words, application is the missing piece. The Word of God won't transform us unless we do what it says. It's like James 1:22-25 says:

> *But don't just listen to God's word. You must do what it says. Otherwise, you are only fooling yourselves. For if you listen to the word and don't obey, it is like glancing at your face in a mirror. You see yourself, walk away, and forget what you look like. But if you look carefully into the perfect law that sets you free, and if you do what it says and don't forget what you heard, then God will bless you for doing it.*

Listening to God's Word without doing what it says is futile. So, if we read God's Word but don't apply it to the areas where we need healing, we won't make much progress. We will be left with a bunch of puzzle pieces but little understanding of where or how they fit into the larger picture of our lives. Here's the thing: as believers, I would venture to say that we know the right answers to many of our problems. And if we don't, we can quickly find Bible verses that speak to our situations. However, healing will not come to your life through information or even revelation. It comes through applying that revelation.

We receive revelation when we go to church, attend Bible studies, and talk to friends. It's a great feeling when we receive answers to problems we have faced before or will face later. We often refer to this as spiritual food. When we listen to a teaching and "eat a spiritual meal," we think it makes us grow. However, receiving revelation is only the first part of getting spiritually fed. In John 4:34 (NKJV), Jesus said, "My food is to do the will of Him who sent Me, and to finish His work." We grow spiritually when we put action to the revelation we received. As I always tell my congregation, "Revelation

It All Boils Down to One Thing

without application is a wasted spiritual meal." You only get the nutrition of that word if you put it into action. If you don't use it, you lose it!

In her book *Switch on Your Brain*, Dr. Caroline Leaf provides the scientific explanation for this phenomenon. A process called protein synthesis helps us store new ideas in our brains. When we learn something new, these proteins only last for 24 to 48 hours—unless the knowledge is applied. Dr. Leaf writes, "Our genetic makeup fluctuates by the minute based on what we are thinking and choosing." If you don't activate revelation within two days of learning it, you lose it!

I propose that most believers have many expired revelations in their heads that were never applied. That's why we can feel passionate and excited when learning something new. However, when we look at our notebooks and review the same information a few weeks later, it feels weak and like the moment is gone. We wonder if anything was real or if we just got caught up in the excitement of the moment. There are a lot of good answers in the body of Christ but very little authority. Why? Because people haven't activated those answers, they don't have real authority to speak on the matter. Therefore, they have a lot of great yet useless puzzle pieces because they are not plugging them in where they belong. They are not living in the full picture that God intended for their lives. The purpose of revelation isn't to feel good or sound smart, it is to be applied. Food is to be eaten, but it is also meant to have nutritional value for our growth and health. Revelation is supposed to be applied, and in turn it produces a testimony. Many people chew spiritual food, but never get the nutritional value that produces growth because they never apply that piece where and when it is needed. This explains why so many Christians who "knew" Psalm 91, quoted it, and had it hung up in a big frame in their living rooms were terrified, locked up, and fearing death during the pandemic. Psalm 91 was head knowledge. It was a high value, but it was not a core value. It wasn't their hearts' belief.

Revelation 12:11 says that we overcome by the blood of the Lamb and the power of our testimony. We defeat the enemy, experience healing, and help others do the same by putting God's Word to work in our lives. One of the first testimonies I can recall happened when

I was 13 years old. I was saving for a $30 BB gun, and when I finally collected that last dollar, I was ready to hightail it to the store. My dad was prepared to take me, but kindly reminded me, "Did you set aside your tithe, son?"

My heart sank. "Uhhh…I don't think so; I won't be able to buy it if I tithe." I fumbled over my words, and the battle was even worse in my mind. I completely forgot about tithing and didn't have the extra three dollars to do so. If I gave 10 percent of my earnings, I would only have $27. I thought it over for a minute and decided to wait to purchase the toy until I had enough money. That Sunday, when I placed my envelope with $3 in the offering plate, it felt like I had passed a test. Later that afternoon, my family and I went into town to walk around the shops. I asked my dad if we could walk by the BB gun store so I could ensure that it was still waiting for me once I had enough cash. To my amazement, when we arrived, the BB gun was on sale for $27! I still remember the way the miraculous, supernatural intervention felt. I know it might seem silly, but I had been looking at that item for six months, and it had never been on sale. This was no coincidence. At that point, I knew for myself that God's Word is true, He is my provider, and that my 90 percent goes further when I honor Him with my tithes. Now no one could ever talk me out of tithing or generously giving offerings. Why? I don't just know the scriptures about tithing. I know for a fact that it works!

Such powerful experiences become part of you. An experience out-teaches any great knowledge.

Trauma is a negative experience that is very much like a testimony. Trauma causes a sort of ditch in the brain, which very quickly and violently teaches us a lesson—kind of like the hot stove example. After the child touches the hot stove he has been repeatedly warned about by his parents, he experiences quick, deep, violent pain that marks him with a new understanding. Don't touch the hot stove, it burns!

Testimonies are the positive outcome of traumas, if we could say it this way. Saul had one of these when he encountered Jesus. He had a violent, traumatic encounter with God that taught him something in a moment, which ended up overruling all the knowledge he had

It All Boils Down to One Thing

accumulated as a Pharisee his whole life. This traumatic experience is what we call salvation. I believe salvation is supposed to be a positively traumatic event where we encounter our Savior Jesus rescuing us from the kingdom of darkness and violently translating us into His Kingdom of light (Colossians 1:13). I believe this can also explain a major difference in people's lives when they get saved, why we see radical change in some and little to no change in many others.

When we apply God's Word to our lives and experience these encounters that produce testimonies, they become part of us, part of our belief systems, part of our hearts. A ditch was created in me that reminds me God is my provider and tithing and sowing is the way to have more than enough for every good work. I was powerfully and positively traumatized by that testimony at age 13 when I experienced what was impossible for me at that moment.

Nobody can ever take your testimony away from you. That is why I am so excited for you to journey with me as we go through this book together. I will show you how to apply the Word of God and co-labor with the Holy Spirit using the timeless practices of prayer, meditation, and declaration. These practices will show you how to identify the broken, painful, and empty places in your life so that you can place the missing puzzle pieces—the Word of God—into the gaps in your life. Third John 1:2 (NKJV) says, "Beloved, I pray that you may prosper in all things and be in health, just as your soul prospers." This book is a tool to help you prosper in all things and heal your life. How? By filling your heart with the pieces Jesus already paid for you to have. It is a blueprint for how you can radically and relationally experience the redemptive healing of God. Through this teaching, I have seen marriages restored, financial breakthroughs, bodies healed, addictions broken, and people flourishing in their God-given purposes. Personally, I have experienced wholehearted physical, mental, and emotional healing. God has miraculously redeemed relationships that I thought were broken forever! You will read several of these stories in this book. My prayer is that you will receive a revelation that will empower you to heal your life!

What Does Healing Really Mean?

Before we get too far, I want to identify what it truly means to be healed. Jesus healed thousands during His earthly ministry, and today, countless people are being healed in His name. Jesus healed on many levels. Yes, people were healed from physical ailments like leprosy, blindness, and even death. However, He didn't stop there. Their souls were healed, too. People who had been rejected and isolated for decades suddenly felt seen, and the outcasts could reenter the community. Ultimately, Jesus paved the way for them to experience a restored relationship with their Heavenly Father.

The same is true for you. When Jesus heals you, it's complete. Your mind, body, spirit, and soul reap the benefits for eternity. Even *Merriam-Webster's Dictionary* defines healing as, "to make free from injury or disease; to make sound or whole."

The Bible tells us in Romans 10:9 that we will be saved when we put our faith in Jesus. That word *saved* is the Greek word *sozo*, and the meaning and implications of this word are far wider than eternity in heaven. It means saved, healed, delivered, and *whole*. Healing means to become whole again. This gives us permission to believe for wholeness in every broken area of our life. In my church, we have a specific ministry that helps people become whole through assisted prayer. We help people hear God's voice, and through the leading of the Holy Spirit, we help people discover the lies they are believing. The lies of the enemy rob us from the full effect of salvation. That's why this ministry is called *sozo*.

Jesus said in John 10:10 that the thief comes to kill, steal, and destroy, and one of the ways he steals is through lying to us and hoping we believe his lies. He has no power over us. He is a defeated foe. The only way he can steal from us is when we believe his lying words. That verse then says that Jesus came that we might have life and life more abundant. Jesus wasn't stuttering; I believe He was referring first to eternal life, which is where most believers stay at, and second, abundant life here on earth. It would be redundant to say life is going to be abundant

It All Boils Down to One Thing

in heaven—we already know that. There's going to be no pain, and the streets are made out of gold. Jesus was saying that through salvation in Him, we have access to abundant life here on earth.

Third John 1:2 tells us that our outward prosperity hinges on the prosperity of our soul, or as I like to say it, the more whole I become inside, the more I will experience prosperity in health, relationships, finances, and all areas of life. When you upgrade your heart, you upgrade your life, because it's in your heart where you store up your core beliefs and produce the life you're living today.

So, when you see me talk about *sozo* later in the book, this is the process of assisted prayer I am referring to.

Healing in your life is about more than getting free from sickness. (Though that is certainly a part of what this book will help you do.) Even more so, the type of healing we are discussing is wholehearted healing. It is freedom from sin, addiction, unhealthy thoughts, unforgiveness, and emotional pain. This level of healing will break toxic and dysfunctional cycles that have been sabotaging you. It will expose and mend the deeply rooted beliefs repelling God's promises from manifesting in your life. Essentially, you will experience the fullness of life for which you were created. This is the kind of healing that makes you whole. When God heals you, you have the capacity to help others heal. As pastor and author Peter Scazzero wrote, "Our first act of love to this world is to let Jesus heal us."

Wholehearted healing starts with accepting Jesus as your Lord and Savior, but it does not end there. So, read this book from the lens of receiving healing in any area where you want to become whole. Apply the lessons to the places where you need a new measure of God's presence, power, and promises.

A quick warning: this book is not a tidy list of religious "to-dos" that you can check off. Instead, it's a relational process that requires deep heart work with God. This book provides a template for healing and freedom, but you and the Holy Spirit will have to fill it with the substance. I can promise you this: you'll never regret doing the heart work in your life. So, let's get started!

Chapter Summary

- It all boils down to one thing—the heart. As Proverbs 4:23 says, "Guard your heart above all else, for it determines the course of your life." The New King James Version puts it like this: "Keep your heart with all diligence, for out of it spring the issues of life."
- When our head knows something but our heart believes something opposite, we call this cognitive dissonance, which is like an internal hypocrisy causing a form of internal war instead of an internal agreement.
- The meaning we give things has a great impact on how our belief system is being shaped, regardless of it being the truth or not.
- Application is the missing piece to breakthrough. Knowing where and when to apply the Word of God is key for becoming whole. A revelation with no application is a wasted spiritual meal.
- Trauma is a shortcut to writing something deeply in our hearts, whether it is positive or negative.
- *Sozo*, the word for *salvation*, means more than eternal life. It also means wholeness; healing physically, emotionally, and in our hearts; and deliverance and restoration in the places of brokenness in our lives. *Sozo* is also what we call one of our ministries in which we help people pray, hear God's voice, and identify lies from the enemy that are robbing us and affecting our heart's belief systems against God's Word.

Activate: Identify

To get the most out of this book, you need to make it personal. Consider the following definition of healing: "to make free from injury or disease; to make sound or whole." Take some time to write down your answers to the following questions:

- Physically, where are you in pain? Where in your body do you need healing? _____

It All Boils Down to One Thing

- Relationally, what friendships or family ties need to be strengthened? _____
- Personally, where are you not experiencing abundant life? _____
- Spiritually, what would you like to have more of in your relationship with God? _____

CHAPTER 2

DOING THE ~~HARD~~ HEART WORK

Have you ever gotten your car stuck in a ditch, in sand, or even worse the mud? In the midst of being stuck, the natural instinct is normally to press the gas pedal harder. Unfortunately, the more you accelerate and spin your wheels, the deeper your vehicle will sink. You might even cause damage to other parts of your car in the process!

When you're stuck, you tend to run faster and harder in the same direction. Frustration creates chaos, and chaos clogs mental clarity. The same is true in your spiritual life. You want to be a good Christian, so you forcefully modify your behaviors to try to attain holiness. This can keep your problems at bay for a while, but it doesn't lead to true and lasting transformation. Spinning your wheels is not sustainable or effective. Over time you will burn out, become bitter, and damage the people around you. Sadly, it's true: hurt people hurt people.

Unfortunately, I know from experience.

I have five amazing children, and I passionately love each one of them. However, as any parent knows, loving your children does not keep you from getting frustrated. We all have our triggers. Before I was a parent, I told myself I would share everything with my kids. I was determined not to be the, "That's mine, don't touch that!" kind of dad. That all changed when my son began to play with my tools and leave them scattered in the garage. He's a really creative kid who loves to build, but many times, he takes apart or even breaks things

Doing the ~~Hard~~ Heart Work

before trying to build. This became a habit for him, and after a long day's work, I would arrive home tired and seeing the tools all over the house would send me into a tailspin. I would raise my voice and say things I came to regret. The conviction would settle in during my quiet time with the Lord later in the evening. I didn't want my anger to squash my son's creativity forever! I would pray things like, "God, please give me strength and help me with my anger." I'd resist the temptation to be angry for a while, but after a few triggering instances, I'd have another outburst. So what was the real solution? Well, I can tell you it is not working harder at the problem but rather doing the heart work to remove the problem from its root. So many Christians live their lives telling themselves and others, "Don't be angry. Don't get angry…" constantly trying to control the flesh and modify their behaviors, but when God showed me I needed to do the heart work, I discovered anger wasn't the problem—it was only a symptom.

The Holy Spirit revealed to me that the root cause for my anger was a lack of patience. We have the greatest gift inside of us, the Holy Spirit. He knows exactly what we need and what is happening in our hearts. I was focusing on anger—the symptom—but not going after the true issue of my heart. After I realized that it was a patience issue, I began to meditate on scriptures that dealt with patience and declared the truth until it became real in my life. Anger then effortlessly went away. See, when I focused on anger, anger was magnified, because what you focus on you get more of. But when I realized it was a patience problem, I meditated on the Holy Spirit's fruit, which was already inside of me. Fruit isn't hard to produce. You just need to cultivate it and it grows. So I grew in patience and continue to do so. I don't need to fight anger, I only need to remind myself I already have the patience that it takes for whatever is in front of me.

The Bible makes it really simple. When you repeatedly experience the same temptation and struggle, you don't have to address a million different issues. Just get to the root in your heart. Proverbs 4:23 (NKJV) is a concept we will repeatedly return to throughout this book. It says, "Keep your heart with all diligence, for out of it spring the issues of life."

Distraction is one of the devil's favorite tools. When you encounter an issue, the enemy will try to overwhelm you with all the external factors. Satan tries to keep us trimming weeds. Nobody trims weeds, they get pulled from the root. Yet, we try fighting the symptoms, numbing the pain, and building systems to control us externally. It's like a dog chasing its own tail. This is how the enemy keeps us exhausted—trying instead of getting to the root. Remember it all boils down to one thing—the heart. Ask the Holy Spirit what the root is in your life, so you're not wasting time trimming weeds and managing symptoms. It's not the hard work that will solve your problems; it's the heart work.

Here's the good news, friend: you don't have to spin your wheels any longer. There is a better way.

Heart transformation doesn't come by force; it is quite the opposite. We receive power by surrendering to the Holy Spirit. And power is better than force any day of the week. Jesus is our prime example. He prayed, He had the Word inside of Him, and when He spoke, power flowed. Many believers pray, meditate, and declare but not much happens when they do. Throughout this book, we will explore prayer, meditation, and declaration in greater depth and discuss how to wield these weapons like Jesus did to experience breakthroughs in every area of life. We will learn how to apply the scripture and truth we are already familiar with to any place that's not experiencing the abundant life Jesus paid for us to have.

But for now, we need to work backward to go forward. We're stuck in some mud, remember?

Uproot, Tear Down, Destroy, and Overthrow

In 1173, an ambitious group of Italians decided to build a bell tower in their city's main square. It stood straight for five years, but when a third floor was added, it began to tilt ever so slightly. The citizens of Pisa were astounded. It became apparent that the clay foundation was not strong enough to keep the tower upright. Due to this problem, construction work on this tower ceased for a cool 100 years.

Faith & Flame · DESTINY IMAGE · HARRISON HOUSE · soundwisdom

NORI MEDIA GROUP
167 Walnut Bottom Rd. Shippensburg, PA 17257

PACKING SLIP

Page	Customer ID	Invoice ID
1	21015	**1177946**
PO #	Batch ID	Ref Date	Order Date
MOM3966091		7/14/2025	7/7/2025

Sold To: Baker & Taylor Books
2810 Colisium Centre Drive, Suite 300
Attn: Accounts Payable
Charlotte, NC 28217

Ship To: Baker & Taylor Books
501 South Gladiolus St
Momence, IL 60954-1799

Customer PO #	Rep	Warehouse	Shipped Via	Terms	Ordered By
MOM3966091	Redmond, Crystal	Main Warehouse	UPS Ground Collect	Net 90 Days	

ProdCode	Title	Location	List Price	Net Price	Ordered	Shipped	Corrected
9781667509396	Radical Healing	E35E	19.990	9.000	1	1	

Less than 500 pounds ship collect UPS

***Over 500 pounds-enter into the TMS and ship using assigned carrier

This is just a portion of instructions- ANY QUESTIONS or Concerns SEE ROUTING GUIDE FOLDER IN SHARE DRIVE

Please ship using UPS collect acct #622320.

Freight: _____

By: _____

Invoice Value	Weight	Total Units Ordered	Total Units This Shipment
9.00	0.45 lbs.	1	1

Doing the ~~Hard~~ Heart Work

A century later, the engineer Giovanni di Simone added more floors to the tower. He tried to balance it by making one side of the floor taller than the other. Then, a seventh floor and a bell tower were added to the project, which caused it to lean even more. The whole construction process lasted roughly 200 years. Though the Leaning Tower of Pisa's foundational issues are the source of its fame, it was prone to collapsing and injuring a lot of people. This danger was so imminent that civil engineers intervened in 1990 to stabilize it.

When we recognize a problem in our lives, the temptation is to move forward as though nothing is wrong. We think that if we persist in our ambitions and continue to build, the issues will go away. This is wishful but naïve thinking. On the contrary, the pressures of life will cause foundational cracks to widen until the imminent collapse occurs. With the Leaning Tower of Pisa, the tower's weight began to diffuse downward until it reached the weakest point of the structure. Similarly, if we don't heal our hearts, the enemy will continue to attack us in our most vulnerable areas.

Here's the ironic part. We often avoid the heart work because we're ignorant or because it appears intimidating. Life is demanding, so it's second nature to buckle up and barrel forward. We don't want to waste time. However, Pisa shows us that this approach is not productive. It actually causes more problems. When you deal with the source of a problem, you can completely uproot it and reach your desired result sooner. However, if you avoid the problem, it will delay God's desired destination for you. God's perfect will for your life includes wholehearted healing and complete restoration. You can choose to partner with that process head-on, or you can ignore the heart work and experience a lot of heartache in return.

Eight hundred years after Pisa's inception, the next generations had to remedy its problems. Engineers suspect it will need another facelift in 200 years or so. Similarly, when we don't deal with our issues, we risk burdening the next generation. On the flip side, you can leave a legacy of freedom when you choose to heal your heart. You can conquer generational giants like anxiety, addiction, poverty, and even illness so that the next generation doesn't have to endure the same battles. What a powerful inheritance to leave!

But before restoration or construction, you must demolish anything getting in the way. Can you imagine what would happen if architects scrapped Pisa the moment they recognized the foundational issue? Instead of a thousand years, the process would have taken less than a decade. Sure, they would have lost money in the short term, but in the long term, millions of dollars would have been saved. (Ignore the fact that we would have also missed out on a quirky national treasure.)

Many Christians are not living in the peace, provision, or promises that they read about in the Bible because they're trying to build on a broken foundation. This can feel incredibly frustrating for people who have been Christians for a while. They wonder why they are not experiencing God's promises while those same promises are being fulfilled left and right for others who just accepted Jesus into their hearts. Some new Christians see, believe, and do miracles that far surpass people who have been believers all their lives. My wife and I see this a lot with Bible school graduates. They're inundated with the knowledge of God's Word but experience very little transformation. At times, this can cause more frustration in them. Knowledge does not equal transformation. The Bible actually tells us that knowledge puffs up.

As a result, many Christians conclude that the Word of God isn't fully true. They end up lowering the Word of God to the level of their experience instead of standing on God's Word and confronting their heart beliefs until their experiences rise to the level of God's Holy Word. People in this situation end up seeing the Bible as relative and God as distant. At worst, they become bitter and frustrated toward God and His church.

So, why does this happen? Why do some people receive breakthroughs sooner than others? Why do love, joy, patience, and the other fruits of the Spirit come easily for some, while it's a battle for others?

As I wrestled in prayer with this question, God showed me Jeremiah 1:9-10:

Then the Lord reached out and touched my mouth and said, "Look, I have put my words in your mouth! Today I appoint you to stand up against nations and kingdoms. Some you must uproot and tear down, destroy and overthrow. Others you must build up and plant."

For context, Jeremiah was a prophet during a really tough time. His people, the Israelites, were engaging in all kinds of idolatrous and sinful acts (including human sacrifice). So God told Jeremiah that He was going to exile the Israelites to the wicked nation of Babylon. Jeremiah's assignment was to root out, pull down, destroy, and overthrow the nations and kingdoms that opposed God in order to build and plant nations and kingdoms that furthered God's will.

This reminds me of the TV show *Fixer Upper*. Joanna Gaines, the star of the show and a talented interior designer, would create the vision of what a home was going to look like once a renovation was completed. But before she could bring that vision to life, there was a very important day—*Demo* Day. There is absolutely no way she could make these houses look like her vision without demo day, no way!

Jeremiah was not a military man; he was a prophet. He did not go into physical combat or attack his enemies with a sword. The only ammunition he had was the Word and favor of God. The same is true for us today. Before we can see God's blessings and promises flourish in our lives, we must destroy the things that oppose His Word. If we want to reign in God's Kingdom with the freedom and power He intended for us, we must demo the junk out of our land.

In time, God promised to "faithfully and wholeheartedly" replant Israel and that He would "never stop doing good for them" (Jeremiah 32:40-41). It is always in God's nature to redeem and restore creation to a right relationship with Him. However, before restoration could take place, some demolition had to be done. For wholehearted renewal to occur, certain practices, mindsets, and heart postures had to be removed from the picture. If you remember, the Israelites still had wrong beliefs, even though they had been set free from Egypt. Just because we, as Christians, have been saved and translated from the kingdom of darkness to God's Kingdom of light, it doesn't mean we are free from wrong beliefs, poverty mentalities, slave attitudes, or limiting and toxic beliefs. Again, I'm not referring to knowing these things but to having them as part of our belief system. These things will still keep us from abundant life.

Isn't it interesting that four out of the six things God told Jeremiah He was going to do involved demolition: uproot, tear down, destroy, and overthrow? Only two were about growth: build and plant.

In Hebrew, the demolition words are pretty intense.

For example, the word for *uproot* is *nâthash*. It means to tear away and completely pull something out by the roots (Strong's H5428). *Destroy* is *'âbad*, and it means to wander away and lose oneself to the point of death (Strong's H6). In some instances, destroying is akin to "being utterly undone with no way to flee."

We have a choice. We can uproot the things in our heart that are opposing the Word of God or have the Word of God uprooted from our hearts. We can destroy the things causing us to wander away from truth or let those things destroy us. These words of destruction used in Jeremiah are letting us know that we must show no tolerance for the beliefs that oppose God and that they must be dealt with by an attitude of violence—the kind you would show a thief caught inside your home in the middle of the night. In the 21st century, this is an entirely foreign concept. The majority of people in our day and age like to ignore hard issues. Culture urges us to pursue digital distraction, self-medicate, numb, and follow "your truth" into whatever feels good. Unfortunately, this cultural climate has seeped into parts of the church.

Your hometown may not be under the constant threat of a physical invasion, but I must clarify, the nations and kingdoms we need to destroy represent the ungodly cultures, the unbiblical beliefs, the thought patterns, the traditions of man, and the idolatry that is trying to get us to conform to this world. So many Christians have already left the biblical worldview and many are sadly in the process of it. There are cultural idols, attitudes, thought patterns, and traditions of men that you must overthrow and not allow into your heart.

In Romans 12:2, Paul speaks to this plainly. He writes, "Don't copy the behavior and customs of this world," and many of these ungodly behaviors and customs were written in our hearts from a

Doing the ~~Hard~~ Heart Work

young age, which is why we might not even know they're there, but the good news is the Holy Spirit does. He knows how, what, when, and in what order to uproot, destroy, overthrow, and demolish the things that are sabotaging us from the inside.

Slow Down and Demo

We need to take notes from the Tower of Pisa. In our eagerness to build something new with God, we cannot neglect our foundation. Often, we don't want to do the prep work because that would involve slowing down. And, to be honest, preparation is not very exciting. Demolition is fun for a while, but it's not long until your arms are sore, your head is covered in drywall, and every bone in your body urges you to quit. A desire to build with a distaste for demolition has caused many ministries and pastors to crumble under the pressure. According to The Francis A. Schaeffer Institute of Church Leadership Development, 75 percent of pastors report being extremely stressed. In a study of over one thousand pastors, 100 percent had a colleague who had left the ministry because of burnout, church conflict, or moral failure.

To build something new, you have to prepare the space. The same is true for healing. Preparation is necessary. Even empty land needs to be leveled before something can be constructed on it. If you don't prepare the land, it is like building a Jenga tower on a pile of fallen blocks. The more you add to the tower, the more unstable it becomes. You will start to crumble.

The Holy Spirit is so amazing because He redeems time and reconstructs everything that has fallen apart. Once you partner with Him to uproot, tear down, destroy, and overthrow, the things you build and plant will actually remain. Like a city planner, you will clear the land and survey how to build in your life. And what are you building? The Kingdom of God. Like a master gardener, you will till the soil and cultivate growth. And what are you growing? The fruit of the Spirit. An abundance of peace, joy, love, patience, gentleness, kindness, faithfulness, self-control, and goodness will result from your efforts. It all starts with getting to the root of what is hindering your healing.

Chapter Summary

- When it comes to healing and spiritual growth, modifying behavior is never a sustainable solution. You don't have to focus on a million different issues; you only have to focus on your heart. Why? Because all the issues in our life, the good and the bad ones, flow from our hearts. As Proverbs 4:23 (NKJV) says, "Keep your heart with all diligence, for out of it spring the issues of life."
- If you deal with a problem at its source, you can completely uproot it and reach your desired result sooner. However, avoiding the problem will delay the destination that God wants to bring you to.
- Before you can plant and build, you need to uproot, tear down, destroy, and overthrow anything that opposes the Word of God in your life.

Activate: Form and Foundation

Ask yourself:

What behavior, bad habit, or addiction have I been trying to change but continue to fail in? What have I tried to modify but feel exhausted by?

Write it down.

Now ask the Holy Spirit:

What beliefs, thought patterns, or habits in my foundation do I need to destroy before I can experience breakthrough and transformation in this area?

CHAPTER 3

THE WORST DAY OF MY LIFE

At the beginning of this book, I told you about the horrible accident I had and how it changed my life, so here's what happened.

One beautiful Saturday morning in April of 2021, my friend Carlos and his son Jordan invited me to ride dirt bikes with them in the desert. For months, we had tried to plan this trip, and our schedules finally coincided. I'm not a very consistent rider, but I'll carefully hop on a motorcycle a handful of times a year. However, by no means am I the type to push the limits or take unnecessary risks. So, on this particular expedition, I let Jordan take the lead. He and Carlos had been on this trail many times, and I was the newbie. I was not about to venture off on my own path! We headed off to a lake about 90 minutes away, gliding over firm ground, rocky soil, sandy terrain, and loose gravel. We went up and down steep hills, and I wasn't having any issues. I felt confident but remained cautious.

When I was a kid, my dad taught me to be courageous while remaining respectful of things that could potentially hurt me. On our beach trips, he always said, "Respect the ocean, even if you're feeling confident." It was a healthy way to have fun and exercise wisdom.

Suddenly, our trio came to a very steep hill—the kind you have to commit to once you start going down it. If you stopped halfway, your bike would fall on you from behind. No accelerating either. You could only brake in first gear. As I followed Jordan downhill, he moved to the left side of the road. I thought, *It's all the same. I'll stay on the right*. However, the reality was that the left and the right side had some drastic differences. My side of the road was dropping fast—two feet, four feet, six feet. Before I knew it, my front tire hit the ground, my steering wheel twisted, and the bike launched me off of a 20-foot drop. My legs got tangled with the steering wheel in the air, and when I landed, the pressure of the bike and the fall forced my knee into a 90-degree angle. I heard a resounding crack as pain shot up my leg, and I couldn't make myself look at it. What I did see was a rusty steel rebar right beside me. If I had landed one foot to the right, I would have been impaled.

The doctors confirmed that I tore every tendon and ligament in my leg except for my ACL. Everything was hanging by skin and muscle. It was undoubtedly the worst physical trauma of my life.

There was no doubt that my body had to heal. One look at me would tell you that. However, I was surprised at how the need for physical healing triggered a need for healing in multiple areas of my life. The wounds inflamed a whole host of other symptoms that I didn't realize I needed to deal with. Fear and hopelessness had a new entry point into my life, and the road to recovery was long. I did not get to go to church for two whole months, and I cried every day because I missed the corporate presence of God so much. My friend Chad's encouragement after the accident still echoes in my mind. In response to my recovery, he said, "It's going to be a lot of *hard* work, but the most important work is the *heart* work."

Perhaps you have experienced a defining event like this. One day, it feels like everything is going just great, and the next day, your life is completely upside down. I'm not going to lie to you. Even though I was a pastor with a great ministry, a healthy family, and more than enough evidence of God's goodness in my life, I fell into a bit of a depression after the accident.

My poor wife, Kara, had to be a full-time mom to our kids and nurse me 24/7. She needed a break and expressed her desire to go to Sedona, Arizona, to spend time with her parents at a vacation rental. Even though this was only about a two-hour drive from where we lived, I was adamant that I couldn't go. At the time, I could barely make it to the physical therapist's office down the road. The reason it was difficult for me to go on a car ride was not necessarily the pain. It was the trauma I was experiencing.

Fear had wedged itself deep into my heart in a way I had never known before. Going to physical therapy required me to sit in our minivan's middle bench with my back against one of the doors. My injured left leg had to be extended and elevated over the seat. I'm a tall guy, so this was a very uncomfortable position! It only took us 15 to 20 minutes to get to the doctor's office, and my wife Kara is an excellent driver. We didn't even have any kids in the car to distract us. Still, five days a week, I sat in the car with my eyes squeezed shut and face pressed against the headrest. It was terrifying, but only because of a new wrong belief that got into my heart through the trauma of the accident. This new belief was whispering in my ear, "Something bad and unexpected could happen right now." If you didn't know any better, you would have thought I was on a death-defying roller coaster. A sharp turn or bumpy stop triggered PTSD from the accident, and my anxiety skyrocketed immediately. So, when my wife suggested going on a road trip with all five of our children, it was out of the question.

Then, the Holy Spirit spoke to my heart and said, "Ben, it's time to deal with this." He reminded me of Chad's words about doing the heart work. So, I called my friends Amy and Chip to ask if they'd come to my house to do a Sozo. (Remember I told you about Sozo in Chapter 1?) As a quick reminder, *sozo* is the Greek word for *salvation*, but Sozo is also a powerful healing and deliverance ministry we do at our church. During a Sozo, you pray with a couple of people who act as facilitators and help you hear God's voice. You allow the Holy Spirit to lead you into the spaces that need to be healed or addressed. I clearly needed healing from the PTSD I was suffering from due to the accident.

Thankfully, my friends accepted my 911 call and helped me pray through the pain. After about an hour of praying, I felt something heavy lift off me. Instantly, the fear that was so real—the fear that kept me gripping the back of a minivan seat and told me I'd never make it on a road trip—was completely gone! I immediately called Kara and said, "Let's go to Sedona! I'm free!" From that moment on, my physical healing accelerated. It was like the spiritual breakthrough and the healing that occurred in my soul removed any resistance against my physical recovery.

In some situations, God heals instantly. I have seen too many instantaneous miracles to say that healing always takes time. I've been to many nations and seen miracles happen right before my eyes. For example, one time I prayed for a line of people during a crusade in Brazil. They all had varying degrees of blindness. One after another, I laid my hands on them, and they were instantly healed. Not a single one failed. Children to fully-grown adults would break down in tears when they realized they could see perfectly. I remember taking prescription glasses home as trophies after that trip because people no longer needed them. On other crusades, people with deaf ears, chronic pain, and flat feet were healed. Dozens of crutches and wheelchairs were left at the altar! Needless to say, I've seen too much. Nobody could ever talk me out of believing that God is still healing and doing instant, creative miracles today all around the world. That's why I was taken by surprise when healing from this dirt bike accident took much longer than I expected.

As much as I love, believe in, and pray for instantaneous miracles, they don't happen in every circumstance. Though there will be black-and-white, night-and-day transformations throughout your journey, those moments are still a part of a larger process that God wants to walk through with you.

Pain is not isolated. It affects every area of your life. But here's the good news: so does healing. God is a wonderful creator. When He crafted humans, He made incredibly complex and interconnected masterpieces. That doesn't mean that healing is complex, though. When you follow the guidance of the Holy Spirit and take it one step at a time, healing is simple.

Living from the Inside

Believe it or not, tree roots show us a lot about how the healing process works. The roots of oak trees can reach to seven times their diameter in width and stretch as far as ten feet in depth. Roots are the food storage systems for trees. So, what's stored in the roots is responsible for these trees' overall health. When their root systems are healthy, oak trees can live for more than 1,000 years.[1]

Similarly, your health is directly related to what your root systems are feeding you. Most pain, injuries, and diseases can be traced to a single cause. Once that root cause is discovered and treated, healing advances at a rapid rate. For example, the root cause of my physical pain from the motorcycle accident was my leg. However, in the grand scheme of things, that wasn't the deepest issue. The Holy Spirit showed me that the root cause of my spiritual and emotional pain was fear. Once I discovered that, I was able to directly combat one thing. Rather than guessing and fighting several symptoms, I could get right to the root.

This is what Proverbs 4:23 means when it says that every issue flows out of the heart. Once you treat internal issues, external results will follow. There is an overwhelming amount of scientific evidence that confirms this. In her book *Switch on Your Brain*, Dr. Caroline Leaf explains that 75 to 98 percent of mental and physical illnesses come from one's thought life.[2] The American Institute of Health estimates that 75 to 90 percent of all visits to primary care physicians are for stress-related problems.[3] We have two modes: our fight or flight mode (sympathetic nervous system) and our healing and regenerative mode (parasympathetic nervous system). In fight or flight mode, our heart rates increase and send more blood, energy, and strength to our muscles rather than other parts of our bodies. God gave us this capability to help us survive dire situations, such as running from danger or saving our kids from oncoming traffic. However, if we are in that mode, we are consequently not in the healing and regenerative mode. God created our bodies to heal themselves, so we want to be in healing and regenerative mode 99 percent of the time!

Many people trigger the fight-or-flight response for situations that are not life and death. Work deadlines, finances, and social media comparison can put us in such a tailspin that we forget that at the end of the day, we are okay. When we live in a state of stress, our immune systems weaken, and we get sick more easily. That's why doing the heart work is so transformational. We have seen people healed from stage-four cancer just by going through this process. That's how tremendous an effect it has on our health.

When you unlock the root causes of pain and dysfunction in your life, healing will truly advance. This is not a discovery you can make by yourself. Working harder and striving to clean out your heart only leads to frustration. Instead, the key to finding and healing root issues is inviting the Holy Spirit into the areas where you keep hitting a wall.

To do this, you must relinquish control. If you're anything like me, you like to know everything and control the process. This feeling expresses itself most during road trips when someone else is driving. In my opinion, the driver is either going too fast or too slow, not stopping for enough road trip snacks or coffees, or taking a route that doesn't make sense. There is a compulsion deep inside of us that wants to choose our destination and direction. With God, we aren't in charge of either. In the healing process, we must come to the end of ourselves and humbly ask God for guidance. When we do, He promises to direct our paths. According to Psalm 32:8, "The Lord says, 'I will guide you along the best pathway for your life. I will advise you and watch over you." Jesus promised that the Holy Spirit will "guide you into all truth" (John 16:13).

To stick with the road trip metaphor, God's path rarely goes from point A to point B. Instead, there are a lot of pit stops in places that weren't in your original plan. You may be on your way from Arizona to Colorado, but God will take you to a beach day in San Diego, a trip to the rodeo in Texas, and a podunk town in Utah you didn't know existed. The unexpected is part of the adventure, and it is especially true with the healing process.

As we discussed, our healing is usually linked to one root cause. However, we don't know how far or how deep that root goes. We are connected to it in an intricate way that is not visible to the naked eye. When you're working on your heart, you'll probably be surprised at what comes up. You will think you're addressing something that came up two months ago when it really started 20 years ago.

The Worst Day of My Life

So, in order to heal one thing you're experiencing today, God might take you to other roots that you didn't know were connected to the primary issue. This is why the guidance of the Holy Spirit is so crucial. God wants to heal every place of brokenness in your life until your heart is whole and complete. He is the God of total breakthrough. However, you must do your part to receive it. After all, Jesus paid it all.

Clearing Your Land

Around 1400 BCE, God gave His chosen people, the Israelites, the most prime real estate in the ancient world. This land was so fruitful that it was said to be flowing with milk and honey. The Israelites couldn't take any credit for the abundance. Deuteronomy 6:10-11 says:

> *It is a land with large, prosperous cities that you did not build. The houses will be richly stocked with goods you did not produce. You will draw water from cisterns you did not dig, and you will eat from vineyards and olive trees you did not plant.*

Even though the Promised Land was a gift of grace, the Israelites still had a role in receiving it. God gave them clear-cut and consistent instructions about what to do when they entered the Promised Land. One of the primary calls to action was clearing out the land of its current residents. God said in Numbers 33:51-53:

> *Give the following instructions to the people of Israel: When you cross the Jordan River into the land of Canaan, you must drive out all the people living there. You must destroy all their carved and molten images and demolish all their pagan shrines. Take possession of the land and settle in it, because I have given it to you to occupy.*

RADICAL HEALING

Why would God ask them to do this? Well, for starters, the people who lived in the Promised Land (the Canaanites, Amorites, Hittites, Jebusites, Hivites, Perizzites, and Girgashites) were bad news. They were immoral, served other gods, and offered child sacrifices. God knows how easily culture influences humans. He warned the Israelites that if they didn't drive out the inhabitants of the land, they'd be "like splinters in your eyes and thorns in your sides. They will harass you in the land where you live" (Numbers 33:55-56). In other words, they would be a huge pain in Israel's backside!

Unfortunately, even though God was so clear in His instructions, the Israelites were half-hearted. They did not drive out all of the original inhabitants of the Promised Land, so these inhabitants corrupted the Israelites for several generations. The Israelites always struggled with this. They were never able to just follow God wholeheartedly. They had compromised, disobeyed, and done a lot of conforming to the world. They married women in the land and continued mixing with nations and kingdoms that did not worship the Lord. Consequently, they adopted many of their mindsets, practices, lifestyles, and lived a less than abundant life because of their unfaithfulness and disobedience to God. I always say, you can't obey someone you don't trust, and when you're forced to, it becomes abuse. The Israelites didn't fully trust God. They thought He was withholding goodness from them, so they disobeyed constantly. Through the period of the judges and then the kings, the Israelites had constant battles with their enemies. King David was one of the good kings, and he continued cleaning the land from enemies like the Jebusites.

Second Samuel 5:6 says that David, "Led his men to Jerusalem to fight against the Jebusites, the original inhabitants of the land who were living there."

The word *Jebusites* translates to "those who trod on; polluted." Evidently, the Jebusites' wicked ways polluted Israel and trod on the people who lived there, making it harder for them to follow the Lord.

When you tolerate something, you empower it. David knew that the Jebusites had to go or they would keep growing. Second Samuel

5:7 documents his success: "But David captured the fortress of Zion, which is now called the City of David."

Smashing Strongholds

To fully enjoy God's will for them in the Promised Land, the Israelites had to clear out everything and everyone who opposed it. Our hearts are similar. Think about it. We have access to the Kingdom of Heaven and the authority to bring it to earth (Matthew 16:19). Yet many Christians surrender that right and let the enemy trample them in their own domain.

The Bible makes it plain that anyone who belongs to Christ has become a new person (2 Corinthians 5:17). However, every Christian knows that our old nature doesn't automatically disappear when we accept Jesus into our hearts. Our spirit is born again, this time from the incorruptible seed (1 Peter 1:23), and it becomes one with the Holy Spirit (1 Corinthians 6:17), and it is perfect, lacking nothing. However, Romans 12:2 tells us that one of the ways in which we experience transformation is through the renewing of our mind. Meaning, we still need to be transformed, perfected, and matured. There is a journey to walk out with the Holy Spirit. We need Him. That's why we need to have a relationship, not a religion. If I have a religion, I have a book of laws; but if I have a relationship, I have someone to walk with me every day and through every situation of my life.

When we are born again, we still might struggle with the same sin, addictions, and thought patterns as before. So, the key is to recognize there is a process of transformation we need to start, with the leading of the Holy Spirit, in order to drive out the original inhabitants of the land of our hearts.

Let me break down this process in a simple way. Thoughts become seeds to our hearts. In order to experience heart transformation instead of just behavior modification, we need to start changing the way we think. At the same time, we need to start identifying the places where it seems hardest to align with God's Word and experience or see it manifested. This will really clue us in to the places where we have strongholds. That way, we will not be going on a wild goose chase. Instead, we'll be led by the Spirit and by observing the fruit in our lives. That's right, we'll look at the evidence, the patterns, the cycles, and the habits that we don't like and that are robbing us from abundant living.

Let me give you a silly example. If you have ever lost the remote control to your fancy smart TV, you might see eye to eye with me on this. You're desperate and don't want to pay $100 for a new remote so you buy a cheap generic one at Walmart. After ten hours of programing it to your TV, the only buttons that work are the power button and the volume! The rest of the functions aren't compatible with each other. The generic remote cannot send the right signal to the fancy TV to do all the super cool things it's built to do! This is what it is like when you're born again. You have a powerful new perfect Spirit (the same Spirit that raised Jesus from the dead), the authority of the name of Jesus, and permission from Jesus Himself to do "greater works than these" (John 14:12 NKJV). However, your current belief system isn't fully compatible with this powerful Holy Spirit. You can do a few things, but you don't yet have access to all the supernatural features that you have inside of you. You're still being transformed. You can't just write the word *settings* on the button and expect it to work. Many people try doing this and expect it to work, but it is only superficial head knowledge. The new belief has to be programmed into the heart so that it can manifest what God already gave us through Jesus and the precious Holy Spirit living inside of us.

When we change the way we think about something and truly believe it and then quickly see it manifested, it's because we probably didn't have any underlying opposing beliefs about that matter. But when we don't see the manifestation after changing the way we think about something, it is most likely we want to believe it but we have some opposing beliefs deeper inside our hearts regarding that matter. These opposing, sometimes unknown beliefs are the strongholds we are talking about. How do we deal with them? According to the apostle Paul, it is war!

> *We are human, but we don't wage war as humans do. We use God's mighty weapons, not worldly weapons, to knock down the strongholds of human reasoning and to destroy false arguments. We destroy every proud obstacle that keeps people from knowing God. We capture their rebellious thoughts and teach them to obey Christ* (2 Corinthians 10:3-5).

According to the scripture, strongholds are obstacles that keep us from knowing truth and knowing God. *Strong's Exhaustive Concordance of the Bible* defines a stronghold as, "A castle or fortress; anything on which one relies" (Strong's G3794). In the ancient world, people hid in strongholds during wartime. These were places of protection that were difficult to tear down. Strongholds were also disguised, so the enemy would have a hard time locating them. Similarly, we have all built "strongholds of human reasoning" that are so hidden we may not even know they exist. Yet, they are so strong that they subconsciously drive most of our decisions and can stand in the way of our breakthroughs.

Strongholds are a collection of thoughts that all agree about something. Each confirming thought or event adds a brick to the stronghold, even if it's false evidence. Let's say someone told you that you were a mistake as a child. Then, your parents got divorced, and the enemy whispered the lie, "See? You are not enough for your dad to stay." As other normal events happened in your life—you didn't get picked for the team, a teacher forgot your name, or a friend rejected you—you began adding more bricks to the stronghold. Eventually, that stronghold would begin to grow on autopilot, and you would find evidence to support the lie on your own. As the smallest things happen, such as a good friend forgetting to text or call you, you automatically assign the false evidence to the stronghold you have been building since you were a child.

Here's an example of how I built (and tore down) one of the most significant strongholds in my life. I grew up in Mexico City. My parents and childhood were wonderful, but we struggled financially. The lack I experienced as a teenager grew into a scarcity mindset. I was always afraid of not having enough. It was hard for me to celebrate other people's blessings and promotions because I did not realize there was enough for everyone. When someone else got blessed, I thought my blessing was gone. When an unexpected expense would surface, fear and anxiety were not far behind. The scarcity mindset became a stronghold that filtered how I saw the world and, more importantly, how I saw God's willingness to provide for me.

Like root systems, strongholds grow deeper and spread further as you feed them new information and beliefs. If you are rooted in the Word of God, you can develop healthy strongholds that keep God close and the enemy far away. However, if you are rooted in the wisdom of the world and find protection apart from God, it becomes increasingly difficult to experience His presence and promises.

Remember, you have the power to "capture their rebellious thoughts and teach them to obey Christ." It's important to note that the scripture says "their" rebellious thoughts. You have the mind of Christ (1 Corinthians 2:16). Thoughts that oppose the Word of God don't belong to you; they are from the enemy. Yet, I see a lot of Christians make the mistake of identifying with the rebellious thoughts as if they are the ones who thought of them in the first place! Here are several examples I've heard from friends and people in my church:

- I don't deserve good things.
- Fear will always be a part of my life.
- I'm too emotional and too much for others to handle.
- I am unlucky or even cursed. Everything I touch breaks.
- I never have enough time.
- Everyone rejects me.
- I am poor and will be poor forever.
- I am sick and my health will decline.
- I can't have what others have. I must watch on the sidelines as others succeed. God will do it for others but not for me.

You build strongholds when you repeatedly rehearse rebellious thoughts. You can tell when a negative thought has become a stronghold when you believe that it's true in your heart of hearts. In other words, you know you are stuck in a bad stronghold when you can't tell the difference between the inhabitants of the land and yourself. The process that we will talk about in the rest of this book—prayer, meditation, and declaration—is how you recognize and get free from those strongholds.

When the Holy Spirit revealed my scarcity mindset, I started to replace the lies with truth. I realized that God had always given me everything I needed, and that He always will. Verses like Philippians 4:19 (NIV) spoke to my heart: "And my God will meet all your needs according to the riches of his glory in Christ Jesus." I learned that when God blesses someone else, it means that He can and wants to do the same thing for me. Acts 10:34 (KJV) helped me solidify this truth in my mind: "God is no respecter of persons."

This transition was not automatic. There was a tension between my old thought patterns and the person I wanted to become. Really, it was a contradiction between the new revelation and the heart beliefs I'd built throughout the course of my life. At the threshold between a new and an old mindset, you must make a conscious choice. Do you want to heal, or do you want to stay in the enemy's stronghold?

Chapter Summary

- The Bible tells us that the issues of life flow from our hearts. If your heart is hurting, it will have a negative impact in your body. Remember that 98 percent of sickness comes from one's thought life.
- Many of your health issues could be traced back to issues of the heart, like mindsets, subconscious beliefs, traumas, or negative memories. Once the real heart issue is treated and healed, physical healing advances at a rapid rate.
- Sometimes you might think the root of the issue is a recent experience only to find out the roots go back years, even decades.

- When we experience toxic cycles, destructive patterns, self-sabotaging situations over the years, it's often due to a stronghold that is directly opposing God's promises for us.
- What you tolerate in your life you empower and grow. If you don't address the "-ites" (the inhabitants of your land) of your heart, they will end up biting you in the back.
- Take negative thoughts captive before they get to your heart. Often, negative thoughts are not your own. They are planted by the enemy who wants to rob God's Word from the soil of your heart.

Activate: Examine Your Roots

Write down the traumas, cycles, and self-sabotaging situations that you know about in your own life.

Write down things you know are unbiblical, yet you continue to do even when you don't want to.

Write down what things you think are the inhabitants of your land—the things you have tolerated that you should've annihilated?

Notes

1 Better Place Forests, "Trees that live the longest," https://www.betterplaceforests.com/blog/trees-that-live-the-longest.
2 Dr. Caroline Leaf, *Switch on Your Brain: The Key to Peak Happiness, Thinking, and Health* (Grand Rapids, MI: Baker Books, 2013), 33.
3 The American Institute of Stress, "America's #1 Health Problem," https://www.stress.org/americas-1-health-problem.

CHAPTER 4

A DIFFERENT KIND OF BATTLE

War isn't the same as it used to be.

In the first century, soldiers fought with spears and swords.

By 1861, the widespread use of rifles, torpedoes, and the telegraph during the American Civil War won it the nickname "The First Modern War."[1]

In 1945, warfare changed forever when the first nuclear bombs were dropped on Hiroshima and Nagasaki, Japan, in World War II.

Since then, the rise of technology has created an even more insidious, hard-to-pin-down battleground. In the U.S. Army paper "The Strategic Environment," commanders explain that, "Battlefields are expanding across all domains, geographic scale, and types of actors."[2] In other words, the fight isn't just on the land, sea, and air anymore. Some threats don't carry guns, and there are hazards that we can't see with our eyes. As technology evolves, there is an increased demand for cyber, robotic, and electronic warfare. Cybersecurity, artificial intelligence, and information technology are growing fields in the military. A good battle plan in the past involved anticipating the enemy's attack and preparing to invade them from several angles. Our modern battlefield requires a more multidimensional approach.

Multidimensional warfare is relatively new in the natural world, but it has been going on in the spiritual realm since the beginning of time. Ephesians 6:12 says, "For we are not fighting against flesh-and-blood enemies, but against evil rulers and authorities of the unseen world, against mighty powers in this dark world, and against evil spirits in the heavenly places." If this process of healing your heart has felt hard or downright impossible at times, there's a good reason. You are on a battlefield, and the war is for your heart.

Unless you are in the armed forces, my guess is that you don't spend a ton of time thinking about how to prevent war or defend yourself against terrorist threats. That's other people's jobs. However, we can't afford to be ignorant of the spiritual warfare that the enemy wages against us every single day. To drive out the original inhabitants of the land, you must be armed and ready.

In this chapter, we will discuss how to renew your mind with the Word of God. Just like a real soldier, one of the first steps to crafting a battle plan is to survey the battlefield. We are fighting against a cultural current that the enemy is using for his advantage.

As humans, we are three-part beings—we are a spirit, we have a soul, and we live in a body. However, most of the time, we only focus on the body. If you've been on a diet, you know how much the body can take over the other two parts. If you give up sweets or cut coffee cold turkey, your body will talk to you and try to convince you to cave. That is why making decisions based on biblical wisdom and the guidance of the Holy Spirit is so important, especially when culture tells us to define reality based on our preferences or emotions. We need to raise our awareness of the spiritual and soulish realms.

Hosea 4:6 (KJV) says, "My people are destroyed for lack of knowledge." The New Living Translation says, "My people are being destroyed because they don't know me." Today, Christians are being destroyed because they don't know the Holy Spirit and are ignorant of the spiritual realm.

The devil didn't give up on you when you got saved; he doubled down. He saw Jesus walking on earth, so he knows what a believing believer (much less millions of them) filled with the Holy Spirit can do. It scares him because he will be in for an early retirement if we start exercising our authority. The enemy isn't concerned with you attending church. What really scares him is when you get filled with the Holy Spirit and realize who God says you are. He really starts sweating when you start believing like Jesus. Sadly, many believers are unbelieving believers, meaning they're not believing correctly.

They might know the right biblical answers but don't believe them. The devil is also not concerned with what you know, but he is concerned with what you believe, because that's when you start manifesting heaven on earth!

John 10:10 calls the devil a thief whose sole purpose is to steal, kill, and destroy. The enemy wants to pull you away from God and steal everything good from your life. He doesn't want you to live in peace, experience joy, or know how powerful you are. He wants you to be sad, bound, sick, broke, and anxious, and he has plotted evil schemes to make that happen. They come in the form of the strongholds we discussed in the last chapter. The devil also steals through lying. If he gets you to believe the wrong things, he steals the right things from you because you can't have what you don't believe. So many people have had their health stolen from them because they believed the enemy's lie that God gave them sickness or that healing isn't for today.

Thankfully, God has given us foolproof weapons that "have divine power to demolish strongholds" (2 Corinthians 10:4 NIV). You can destroy, uproot, overthrow, and tear down every lie and scheme the enemy plots against you. Second Corinthians 10:5 (NIV) goes on to say, "We demolish arguments and every pretension that sets itself up against the knowledge of God, and we take captive every thought to make it obedient to Christ."

The enemy has waged war against our thoughts, and the battlefield is in our minds. So, our battle plan is to:

1. Consistently take inventory of our thoughts and emotions
2. Identify lies
3. Disown and reject the lies and renounce previous agreements with them
4. Replace the lies with biblical truth

Our thoughts can open doors or close doors; they either resist the enemy or give him a foothold in our lives. So, the goal is to capture rebellious thoughts before they get to the heart. At first, these thoughts may not feel out of the ordinary. The devil does not tempt us with desires that are completely out of left field. If you have never stolen anything in your life, I don't think he will waste his time trying to tempt you with the idea of robbing a bank. The devil does not come to a healthy, sober person trying to convince them to do meth. No!

Instead, temptation happens one compromise at a time. Let's say that a suggestive photo pops up on social media, and you stare for a little too long. A week later, you feel a pull to look up similar images online. If you keep giving in to similar temptations, the rabbit trail leads to watching things you would have never considered viewing before that first photo appeared. Every time you give in, the feeling of shame compounds. You can nip shame in the bud by recognizing that those rebellious thoughts were never yours to begin with.

What do I mean by that? The enemy throws darts of fire at you in the form of thoughts. These negative, fearful, sinful thoughts cross your mind, and if you think they're your thoughts, then the devil accuses you of having them and brings shame and condemnation to you. The fiery darts might keep coming, but remember you have the mind of Christ. Therefore, those thoughts aren't yours, so don't agree with them.

The Power of Your Agreement

Negative thoughts are not from God, and they are often not from you either. Lies are from the devil, and you can choose whether or not to agree with them. Here is what Jesus had to say about the devil:

> *He was a murderer from the beginning. He has always hated the truth, because there is no truth in him. When he lies, it is consistent with his character; for he is a liar and the father of lies* (John 8:44).

So, being able to discern the voice of God from the voice of the enemy is crucial. First and foremost, the enemy will attack how you see yourself. His strategy is exposed in Genesis 3 when he tempted Eve in the Garden of Eden. It involves:

Deception

The first thing the enemy did was cause Eve to question God's goodness. He asked, "Did God really say you must not eat the fruit from any of the trees in the garden?" (Genesis 3:1), as if God was withholding something good from her.

Disempowerment

Next, the enemy made Eve question her identity. He told her, "You will be like God," when she was already made in His likeness and image (Genesis 3:5).

Division

Eve gave into temptation, and she and Adam were banished from the Garden of Eden (Genesis 3:23). The enemy's strategy will always try to isolate you from God and people.

The enemy plants thoughts in our minds the way crooks plant false evidence. Then, he will deceive you into thinking that you devised the thought and that you are the bad one. For example, the enemy will plant an idea like "Go sleep around; everyone is doing it." In response, you may think, "Huh, maybe sex outside of marriage is not as big of a deal as they made it out to be in church. Could be fun." Then, even if you didn't act on it, you feel shame as if the original thought was your own, and you are stuck with the idea as if it were. And to make matters worse, you attach this to your identity and start thinking of yourself as an adulterer and a pervert.

Your agreement has power. Whenever you agree with a thought that does not align with the Word of God, you add another brick to a stronghold that protects the lies and keeps out truth. Think about it. When you agree with someone, you have something in common with them. That is why it is crucial to agree with God's voice, not the enemy's. You are a child of God, which means that no other voice should define you except His.

Jesus said things that empower us, told us how He saw us, and what we could do, like these:

> *I will give you the keys of the Kingdom of Heaven* (Matthew 16:19).

> *I tell you the truth, anyone who believes in me will do the same works I have done, and even greater works, because I am going to be with the Father* (John 14:12).

> *Ask me for anything in my name, and I will do it!* (John 14:14)

Our plan to overcome the enemy's strategies starts by changing the way we think. Rather than conforming to a culture that strays further away from reality, we are called to claim truth. Instead of identifying with sadness and pessimism, we are people who believe in the best and renew our minds with hope.

You are set apart for the glory of God. Let's return to Romans 12:2, which says, "Don't copy the behavior and customs of this world, but let God transform you into a new person by changing the way you think. Then you will learn to know God's will for you, which is good and pleasing and perfect." The New King James Version says, "Be transformed by the renewing of your mind."

The Greek word for *renewing* is *anakainōsis*, and one of its translations is, "a complete change for the better" (Strong's G342). Past trauma, shame, or destructive memories and thought patterns do not have to define you forever. You can completely change and know God's perfect will for your life! The question is, how?

To put it simply, renewing your mind is as straightforward as replacing the lies and negativity with life-giving biblical truths. Scripture and science alike back up this fact.

The Science Behind Renewing Your Mind

When God created you, He programmed the power to renew your mind into your biology. Two scientific realities, neuroplasticity and epigenetics, prove this. Neuroplasticity is how our brains constantly grow and change on a structural level. The health research database Physiopedia explains that neuroplasticity is, "The lifelong capacity of the brain to change and rewire itself in response to the stimulation of learning and experience."[3] In other words, what we think about and practice the most will grow and take up mental real estate in our brains.

Let's say that you want to become an expert painter. As you practice your craft consistently, your brain will grow and develop. Neuroplasticity will work in your favor, and your paintings will become masterpieces! On the flip side, neuroplasticity can work against you. Let's say that you experience a traumatic event and ruminate on it over and over. As you do, that memory will wire deeper into your brain, becoming the primary filter and disordering normal functions. Internal thoughts, actions, and reactions have external power. In his book *Live No Lies*, Pastor John Mark Comer explained it like this, "When we believe lies—ideas that are not congruent with the reality of God's wise and loving design—and then, tragically, open our bodies to those lies and let them into our muscle memories, we allow an ideological cancer to infect our souls. We live at odds with reality, and as a result we struggle to thrive."

A fascinating field called epigenetics illustrates this point even further. As defined by The Centers for Disease Control, epigenetics is the study of how your behaviors and environment can cause changes that affect how your genes work. The choices you make and the thoughts you think have the power to switch genes on or off. According to Dr. Caroline Leaf, this scientific revelation shows that we, in a sense, have the power to "do our own brain surgery." Though you may have a genetic predisposition to certain diseases or mental health issues, you can deactivate those genes with your thoughts and behaviors. This explains why identical twins can still have differences, like how one can develop bipolar disorder while the other does not. Dr. Caroline Leaf explains:

> They have the same genome, so they should respond the same way, but their individual perception of the world as well as their ability to choose means they think and react differently, which alters their genetic expression. Although their genes are the same, their patterns of expression can be tweaked through the signal. And this signal is mainly affected by our reaction to the events and circumstances of life.

Your thoughts, reactions, and decisions following certain events in your life can activate or deactivate any generational issues you may be predisposed to. This discovery has major implications. Neuroplasticity means that we can confidently hope that God will totally transform the way we think. Epigenetics proves that we can experience deep healing in the areas that we thought would always be painful and dark.

So, renewing your mind is important. Your thoughts will determine your health and affect the health of those closest to you. Taking authority over your thought life is the very thing that will empower you to experience the fullness of God's plans, purposes, and promises for your life.

For the rest of this book, we are going to take a deep dive into how to heal your heart—your deepest subconscious beliefs—by renewing your mind to the Word of God. This prescription has three simple components: prayer, meditation, and declaration. So, the next chapter will focus on how to uproot, destroy, tear down, and overthrow anything that opposes the Word of God through prayer. You will learn how to identify the strongholds and inhabitants in your land through the power of the Holy Spirit.

Chapter Summary

- There are ideas and values running rampant in our culture that oppose the Word of God.

- According to Ephesians 6:12, we are in a spiritual war. The battle starts in our minds.
- Our thoughts can open or close doors; they either resist the enemy or give him a foothold into our lives. So, the goal is to capture rebellious thoughts before they get into our hearts.
- Oftentimes, negative thoughts and lies don't originate from us. The enemy plants them in our minds, but we have the choice of whether or not to agree with them. Every time you agree with a thought that does not align with the Word of God, you are adding another brick to a stronghold that keeps out the truth. You are making an agreement with the devil, the father of lies, and allowing his words to have authority over your life instead of God's.
- Our strategy against the plans of the enemy starts with changing the way we think. Rather than conforming to a culture that's straying further from the truth, we are called to love and follow the truth. Truth's name is Jesus (John 14:6).
- The study of neuroplasticity and epigenetics has revealed that Romans 12:2 is literal. We can stop generational curses by changing the way we think—God can help us totally transform our belief systems! As a result, we can become fully whole again and live as though trauma, pain, and lifelong toxic habits never happened.

Activation: Take inventory

Ask yourself the following questions and write down the answers.

1. What are some main thoughts you tend to have every day that are negative about yourself?
2. If they didn't come from God, they probably came from the enemy. Which of these thoughts have you come to agree with?
3. Identify the repeated thoughts or mindsets in your life that are not serving you.

Notes

1. Virginia Museum of History & Culture, "The First Modern War?" https://virginiahistory.org/learn/first-modern-war.
2. U.S. Army, "The Strategic Environment," https://www.army.mil/publications.
3. Physiopedia, "Neuroplasticity," https://www.physio-pedia.com/Neuroplasticity.

CHAPTER 5

PRAYING TO UPROOT

Jeremiah 1:9-10 says, "Look, I have put my words in your mouth! Today I appoint you to stand up against nations and kingdoms. Some you must *uproot* and *tear down, destroy* and *overthrow*. Others you must build up and plant."

As we discussed in Chapter 2, this passage includes four demolition and preparation words (uproot, tear down, overthrow, and destroy) and only two constructive words (plant and build). Readying the place where we are going to build is often more important than starting the building process. Before you begin building up and planting seeds, you must prepare the soil. So, suppose you are not experiencing healing or receiving the promises of God in an area of your life. In that case, it probably has more to do with a stronghold, toxic belief, or negative mentality you have not uprooted than an action you have not done.

We can receive new revelation from the Word of God and understand it consciously in our intellect. However, if we want the revelation to transform and shape us, we must plant it so deeply that it affects us at a heart level—in other words, it becomes second nature to us. When a new revelation takes root and displaces a previous toxic belief, you'll see the effects of it on three levels:

1. The way you think
2. The way you speak
3. How you react

That's right, the revelation will become so integrated into your life that you will change on a subconscious level. You'll see the fruit of it as you observe the changes in your default reactions. Jesus reiterated that with every sermon and story He taught, one in particular was crucial for understanding all of them. We have come to know it as the Parable of the Sower, and it illustrates how to live a meaningful and fruitful life.

> *Listen! A farmer went out to plant some seed. As he scattered it across his field, some of the seed fell on a footpath, and the birds came and ate it. Other seed fell on shallow soil with underlying rock. The seed sprouted quickly because the soil was shallow. But the plant soon wilted under the hot sun, and since it didn't have deep roots, it died. Other seed fell among thorns that grew up and choked out the tender plants so they produced no grain. Still other seeds fell on fertile soil, and they sprouted, grew, and produced a crop that was thirty, sixty, and even a hundred times as much as had been planted!* (Mark 4:3-8)

Later, Jesus explained to His disciples that the seed represented the Word of God and the soil indicated the substance of people's hearts. Whether it is lies from the devil, problems and persecution, or the desire for wealth and comfort, many things compete for real estate in the soil of our souls.

Typically, we have more knowledge (seeds) than we know what to do with. By itself, knowledge puffs us up and can inflate our pride. We can know what scripture says but be unaware of how to apply it to our lives. In response to the Parable of the Sower, Andrew Wommack explains, "The Word of God contains total power, but it has to be planted in our hearts and allowed to germinate before it releases that power. The Word was the same in each situation. It was good seed—incorruptible seed (1 Peter 1:23)—but there were different results in each case because of the condition of people's hearts."[1]

This is great news. God is no respecter of persons, and if He does something for one person, He can do it for you. You should read the

Bible through a lens of transformation, not information. Every time you read a verse, picture it like a seed going into your heart. You can expect it to grow and become true for you. If you read the Bible and there is no change in certain areas of your life, then you need to reevaluate your heart's condition.

There is an obvious tension here. Seeds take time to grow. In the waiting, you must also put your faith to work. Andrew Wommack wrote, "The Word does not work for everyone because not everyone will allow the Word of God to work. What would happen if you planted a seed in your garden and dug it up each morning to see what was happening? It would die and never produce fruit."[3]

The seed of God's Word was never the issue. It's the condition of the soil that determines whether or not something will grow. The seed is good, so if the soil is too, it's only a matter of time until the Word produces fruit in your life. As Isaiah 55:11 says, "It is the same with my word. I send it out, and it always produces fruit. It will accomplish all I want it to, and it will prosper everywhere I send it." The question is, will the Word produce a harvest in your life, or will God have to look for another vessel? Remember, one of the main reasons the Israelites did not prosper in the Promised Land as God had intended was because they did not clear the land of its pagan inhabitants. So, if you conform to the worldly culture, it will surely affect your Promised Land experience as well.

Thankfully, you have everything you need to cultivate good soil and have an exceptionally productive and purposeful life. Mark 4:20 can be true for you:

> *And the seed that fell on good soil represents those who hear and accept God's word and produce a harvest of thirty, sixty, or even a hundred times as much as had been planted!*

So, how do you become the type of person whose life produces a one hundredfold return? How do you prepare the land of your heart to receive the living Word of God? By doing the "demo" work! You must uproot, tear down, destroy, and overthrow the unbiblical beliefs, negative images, destructive memories, past hurts, and traumas that have contaminated the soil of your heart. But how do you do that practically?

The answer is prayer.

But not just any kind of prayer. I'm not talking about begging God to cultivate the soil of your heart. Instead, I'm talking about the type of prayer where you co-labor with the God who created you, who knows your innermost being and knit you together in your mother's womb (Psalm 139:13). This kind of prayer is communion with the God who knows you better than you know yourself and can make you whole again.

So, there is a lot to say about prayer, but this chapter will focus on how to use prayer to expose and uproot the negative strongholds hiding in your heart. Without prayer, it is impossible to receive direction from the Holy Spirit. Without direction from the Holy Spirit, we cannot identify the things that are holding us back from breakthrough.

Prayer is the entry point for God to transform your old ways into your new nature in Christ. Prayer is how you survey the land to identify any unwelcome inhabitants—your cultural defaults and ways of being tied to your flesh. It is also our primary tool for uprooting, overthrowing, tearing down, and destroying any negative images, unhealthy beliefs, and destructive memories that are hindering our healing.

How *Not* to Pray

The Baptist church I grew up in hosted regular prayer nights. As a kid, I dreaded these meetings. First, I had to pray on my knees, which often lulled me to sleep. Second, the meetings lasted for hours. Third, the members of the church did not pray in tongues, so I ran out of content to pray about in the first 30 minutes.

Ritualistic prayer is common in religious circles, and it is the very thing that Jesus instructed against. For instance, Catholics pray a set of predetermined prayers on rosaries. Christians of any denomination

Praying to Uproot

can fall into the pattern of praying and reading the Bible to check it off the list rather than to connect with God. When we especially want something from God—a loved one is sick or a career change is needed—we can start to believe that our prayers will work better if we just say them more frequently. Jesus blatantly rejects this idea. Our prayers are not answered by repeating our words again and again.

Don't get me wrong. I have nothing against praying long or on my knees, but the issue is whether or not I am praying from the heart.

Before Jesus taught people how to pray, he taught them how *not* to pray. He instructed, "When you pray, don't babble on and on as the Gentiles do. They think their prayers are answered merely by repeating their words again and again. Don't be like them, for your Father knows exactly what you need even before you ask him!" (Matthew 6:7-8). First and foremost, prayer is about engaging your heart. God cares more about the quality of your prayers than the quantity.

Prayer is *not*:

- Checking a box enough times that it moves God to do something
- Crafting the right words in order to convince God to give you what you want
- Being good enough in the moment you pray to earn God's answers to your prayers

You cannot manipulate God. He sees the heart and is moved by faith. Therefore, our prayers must have faith. When we pray, we must believe that it is God's will to do what we are asking Him to do. We cannot ask God to heal us if we are not sure that it is His will to heal us. We cannot pray for someone else's healing if we believe God may be teaching them a lesson and is possibly causing the sickness to test them. These words from preacher Jesse Duplantis live rent-free in my mind: "You cannot have what you speak against." Before I pray for something, I have to know that it is God's Word and, therefore, His will. Your prayers do not have to sound super spiritual or be long. Short and straightforward prayers can be extremely powerful.

What Prayer Is

First of all, prayer is pure. It needs to be aligned with your heart, not just your head. It is more important that your prayer is honest than to just say the right words. We can't allow room for internal contradictions, which is what causes cognitive dissonance. Instead, you must be single-minded. James 1:6-8 (NKJV) speaks directly to this:

> *But let him ask in faith, with no doubting, for he who doubts is like a wave of the sea driven and tossed by the wind. For let not that man suppose that he will receive anything from the Lord; he is a double-minded man, unstable in all his ways.*

The Bible teaches the power of agreement, and in this scripture, it is saying that the first person you need to be in agreement with is yourself. Why? Because you can want something in your head but believe something different in your heart. This problem occurs because you are a three-part being. God is saying that you are more powerful when you are lined up inside and lined up with His Word. This is another form of a three-cord strand that cannot be easily broken (Ecclesiastes 4:12). Many people easily break because they're not even in agreement with themselves. They want to be in agreement with the Word but they're divided inside, and we know that a house divided against itself will fall (Mark 3:25).

So, an honest prayer is more powerful than a prayer with the "right words." Remember the man in Mark 9:24? He was honest. He said, "I believe, but help my unbelief." That is also a prayer.

Remember that in its simplest form, prayer is talking with God. God already knows everything, and He's not an ATM machine, wishing well, or genie in a bottle. He is a relational God who wants to walk with you daily.

Proverbs 3:5-6 says, "Trust in the Lord with all your heart; do not depend on your own understanding. Seek his will in all you do, and he will show you which path to take." In other words, God is inviting you into a daily relationship where you can ask Him about every decision, big and small. Unlike many of the important, busy people in society who wouldn't give you the time of day, God has all the time in the world for you. Sadly, many religious believers live and pray in a way as if to say, "God, just give me a map or a rulebook, and I'll see You in heaven." However, Jesus invited His disciples to follow Him step by step. The same invitation waits for you today, and prayer is a way to accept it.

So, the first step to healing is to pray from and for your heart. Jesus gave the disciples a prayer that demonstrates this perfectly. Today, we call that template the Lord's Prayer, and it's found in Matthew 6:9-13.

> *Our Father in heaven, may your name be kept holy. May your Kingdom come soon. May your will be done on earth, as it is in heaven. Give us today the food we need, and forgive us our sins, as we have forgiven those who sin against us. And don't let us yield to temptation, but rescue us from the evil one.*

Again, the power is not in words but in the faith and heart connection you put behind them. As you say each sentence, get honest with God about your life. Talk to Him about where you feel stuck or are hurting. Roughly half of the prayer emphasizes praying from the heart, and the other portion asserts the importance of praying for your heart.

Pray *from* the Heart

What I mean when I say "from the heart" is don't babble on and make sure you have the right motive as instructed in Matthew 6:5-7. Jesus told us how not to pray right before He gave us this powerful and simple prayer model in Matthew 6:9. He was giving us an example, a template, which included:

1. Permission to address Him as our Father, wow! How you see God determines your ability to receive from Him. Jesus wanted

to make sure you knew that you were not begging from a distant God but talking with your perfect Dad.
2. Worship and gratitude unto God. This would help us keep the right perspective regardless of what we're praying for and how difficult of a situation it may be.
3. The reminder that we are agents of heaven and our assignment includes occupying till He comes, bringing heaven to earth, and representing our Father and Jesus to this world.
4. Instructions to ask for our needs and the things we desire even when He already knows.
5. Keeping a repentant heart. God knows we will fail and mess up sometimes, and although those sins are paid for and covered by the blood of Jesus, we still need to repent, not because we're unsure of whether or not He'll forgive us (He already did) but because it means we're turning around and acknowledging we fell short and we're doing something to not fall into that again.
6. A reminder of our job to keep our hearts free from offense so that we don't stay broken. Remember that forgiving others doesn't make them right, it makes you whole.
7. Praying for protection.

"Our Father in heaven, may your name be kept holy."

For Jesus, prayer began with worship. In the same breath, Jesus acknowledged God's authority and recognized the intimacy of their relationship. Before Jesus, nobody dared to call God "Father" or even knew they could.

Jesus pioneered our relationship with God. Now, we can confidently pray from our hearts, knowing that He hears us and answers us with the kindness and wisdom of a perfect Father. When we address God as Holy Father, we are saying, "God, You know me better than I know myself. I need You to search my heart for the things that I don't even know are there." (We will explore this more in Chapter 8!)

"May your Kingdom come soon. May your will be done on earth, as it is in heaven."

Next, Jesus prayed in a way that aligned His desires with God's desires. "May your Kingdom come, may your will be done" involves caring about what God cares about. To be candid, praying for the whole earth can seem like the opposite of praying from our hearts. We can say the words, but they feel distant. We can personalize this part of the prayer by replacing "on earth" with specific areas of our lives. For example:

- *May Your will be done in my daughter's school as it is in heaven.*
- *May Your will be done in my local government as it is in heaven.*
- *May your will be done in my coworker's life as it is in heaven.*

This prayer gets to the core of our assignment on earth: to occupy territory and express the Kingdom of God in every area of life.

Jesus was perfect, but we are not. We have desires that do not align with God's will. This portion of the Lord's Prayer can serve as an invitation to humble ourselves before God and pray for His desires. We can pray *for* our hearts—that our desires will become like God's—so that we can truly pray *from* our hearts in alignment with God's will.

"Give us today the food we need."

What do you need today? What do you want but feel like it's too insignificant to ask God for? Jesus empathized with our humanity and God's will to take care of every one of our needs. Many people stagnate in their healing process because they stop at this part of prayer and never talk to God about what is actually bothering them. Even though they meditate on their desires often, they do not invite God into their deepest needs. Remember, God values a short, raw, and vulnerable prayer more than a spiritual-sounding, elaborate prayer detached from your heart. As C.S. Lewis once said, "We must lay before Him what is in us, not what ought to be in us."[3]

> "And forgive us our sins, as we have forgiven those who sin against us. And don't let us yield to temptation, but rescue us from the evil one."

In the conclusion of His prayer, Jesus demonstrated how to cultivate our hearts through prayer. Every day, we do three things: experience temptation, sin, and come into contact with people. People have the propensity to hurt or disappoint us. We can become offended when they do, and offense is a breeding ground for unforgiveness.

Sin, shame, and offense can stick to our hearts, and falling into temptation can become habitual. So, as Jesus showed us, praying for our hearts is essential. These kinds of prayers can cleanse us from our sins, free us from unforgiveness, and rescue us from the enemy.

Many times, we pray for our needs, wants, careers, friends, family, government, and global issues. These are great things to pray about. However, how often do we direct our prayers toward our own hearts? When was the last time you prayed for your soul? As much as we pray about external issues, we need to pray about internal issues as well, especially because every issue flows from the heart!

So, if God knows everything we need, why do we pray? When it comes to our hearts, praying is a way for us to agree with the Holy Spirit. When we say, "Amen," we are literally declaring, "Let it be so," to God's will for our lives.

Praying for our hearts can be uncomfortable because it involves taking a hard look in the mirror and being vulnerable. We all have parts of our hearts that do not line up with the Word of God, and they affect our actions more than we think. My wife and I pray Proverbs 30:8 from *The Passion Translation* every day, and it is an audacious prayer: "Empty out of my heart everything that is false—every lie, and every crooked thing."

When we started praying this way, we saw effortless, spontaneous breakthroughs happen in different areas of our lives. Suddenly it was easier to stay humble, be selfless, and take responsibility without feeling shame or condemnation. If people tell me that they want a better marriage, I encourage them to work on their hearts. Most marriage issues aren't marriage issues; they are personal issues rooted in the heart. When people choose to deal with these "heart issues," their lives naturally improve.

Proverbs 30:8 gives the Holy Spirit permission to course-correct every place that is crooked, right down to the slightest of distortions. There are dark corners in our hearts that we can't see without the light of God. We all have sins of ignorance that can keep us from wholehearted healing. We are quick to notice the external results in our lives that we do not like—the anger, the addiction, the sickness, the struggling bank account—but we do not always recognize the heart issues that caused these external results to spring up in the first place. That is when Ephesians 1:18 comes into play as another great prayer to adopt:

I pray that your hearts will be flooded with light so that you can understand the confident hope he has given to those he called— his holy people who are his rich and glorious inheritance.

When light floods your heart, everything is exposed. The lies, sins, and issues you did not previously notice appear in plain sight. So, when you pray, "Lord, flood my heart with light," you will gain understanding, confident hope, and revelation.

Pray to be Made Complete

Do you ever feel like something is missing? Maybe you are searching for an answer, longing for a dream, or desperately needing peace. When we dwell in places of lack for any length of time, it can feel like there is a gaping hole in our hearts. Ephesians 3:19 offers the remedy to this deficiency:

May you experience the love of Christ, though it is too great to understand fully. Then you will be made complete with all the fullness of life and power that comes from God.

In the original Greek, the word *complete* is *plērōma*. It translates to "fullness, fulfilling." Here are a few examples of how the New Testament uses *plērōma*:

- That which is (has been) filled
- The body of believers, as that which is filled with the presence, power, agency, riches of God and of Christ
- Completeness or fullness of time

As you clear the land of your heart, you can look forward to this fullness. When you destroy, overthrow, demolish, and uproot the things that are inconsistent with the Word of God, you create the space to be filled with God's presence, power, agency, and riches. I guarantee that is better than any old junk you have been holding on to.

God designed our hearts to be filled with His love. According to Ephesians 3:19, experiencing this love is the key to satisfaction and completeness. When we experience supernatural love, our lives burst with fullness and beam with God's power! In fact, experiencing God's love is how we live in the fullness that Jesus talks about in John 10:10 (NIV): "The thief comes only to steal and kill and destroy; I have come that they may have life, and have it to the full." We can't fully experience God's love in this life, but we can experience it more with every passing day. Being complete means overflowing with abundance yet always hungering for more of God. We are full, and we are being filled. That's a full-filling life!

I pray the promise of Ephesians 3:19 over myself, my wife, and my children daily. Yes, I want my kids to have good friends. Yes, I want my kids to be prosperous and healthy. But above all, I want them to be complete and whole in their hearts. If they are whole in their hearts (rather than having holes in their hearts), it will determine how everything else in their lives goes. Our hearts will determine what we attract, what we keep, and what grows.

Guard Your Heart

Just like you're now learning to pray for your heart and partner with the Holy Spirit to cultivate the land of your heart, do the same to protect it and keep it whole.

Praying to Uproot

Proverbs 4:23 (NIV) instructs, "Above all else, guard your heart, for everything you do flows from it." Before Jesus came onto the scene, it was up to the Jews to guard their own hearts. This is a huge burden to bear alone. Everything we do and every issue of our life hinges on guarding our hearts. Without guidance from the Holy Spirit, the Jews inevitably fell short. When considering my own life, there are so many mistakes I would have made and wrong paths I would have taken if the Holy Spirit had not led the way. There would be so much that I never healed from, too.

Because of Jesus, we no longer have to guard our hearts alone. Philippians 4:6-7 says, "Don't worry about anything; instead, pray about everything. Tell God what you need, and thank him for all he has done. Then you will experience God's peace, which exceeds anything we can understand. His peace will guard your hearts and minds as you live in Christ Jesus."

God's peace will guard our hearts and minds! This is the joy of our salvation. We aren't left alone and can experience God's best in this life and for eternity. We have a 24/7 guard who will protect the very thing inside of us from which every issue of life flows.

In the original Greek, the word *guard* is translated from *phroureō*, which means "to guard, protect by a military guard, either to prevent hostile invasion, or to keep the inhabitants of a besieged city from flight." In other words, the peace of God will guard the godly strongholds you build. That way, any hostile invasions from the enemy will not come close to entering your heart or mind.

Philippians 4:7 gives us the blueprint for how to access this guard:

1. Don't worry about anything.
2. Pray about everything.
3. Tell God what you need.
4. Thank Him for what He has done.

It's that simple! As God's peace guards you, chaos will turn into clarity. He will expose the enemy's strategies. This is your defensive strategy, but you also need an offensive one.

Pray to Demolish and Clean Up

If you have ever watched a home remodeling show, you know that "demo day" is a key part of the process. Before the magic can happen, unwanted walls must be smashed, and old structures must be gutted.

Typically, people love demo day. The camera shows people laughing as they smash hammers on outdated cabinetry and throw sledgehammers on loose pieces of drywall. However, the footage rarely shows the clean-up process that inevitably follows.

We love the high of demolition—the adrenaline that comes when God speaks and reveals things to us. God has a way of making the Sword of the Spirit feel good, even when it sharply convicts the hidden corners of our hearts. However, after the demolition, we have to be diligent about cleaning up the mess.

As you pray, God will reveal any root issues that are stuck in the soil of your heart—sin, strongholds, and limiting beliefs that you need to uproot. The next step is to clean up the mess so that the Word of God has room to work in your life.

If you don't, it will be like living in a chaotic construction zone. Imagine trying to eat a delicious meal that has crunchy bits of your ceiling in it. You could not enjoy the taste or reap the nutritional benefits! That is what it can be like when we try to digest the Word of God without dealing with our mess first.

Once we remove the junk from our hearts, we have to fill the gaps with truth. Otherwise, there is space for the same old stuff to return. Meditating on scripture is how we plant the right seeds. As truth replaces lies, God's Word will produce a harvest of 30, 60, or 100 times in our lives!

Chapter Summary

- When it comes to healing, external solutions alone won't cut it. Healing requires uprooting the thing that's harming you once and

Praying to Uproot

for all. Otherwise, it's like trimming down weeds and expecting them to go away. They need to be plucked out from the root.
- We should read the Bible through a lens of transformation, not information. Every time we read a verse we can picture it like a seed going into our hearts. We expect it to grow and become true in our lives. If we read the Bible and there is no change in certain areas of our lives, then we need to reevaluate how we are reading the Bible. We need to be able to see ourselves in God's promises and imagine the promises being fulfilled in our lives.
- Prayer is how we survey the land of our heart to identify any unwelcomed inhabitants—our cultural defaults and ways of being that are tied to our flesh. It is also our primary tool for uprooting, overthrowing, tearing down, and destroying any negative images, unhealthy beliefs, and destructive memories that are hindering our healing.
- Effective prayer involves praying *from* our heart and praying *for* our heart.
- When you uproot the things that are inconsistent with the Word of God, you create the space to be filled with "the fullness of life and power that comes from God" (Ephesians 3:19).

Activate: Prayer Challenge!

The Bible has several prayers you can adopt to pray for your heart. I encourage you to pray Proverbs 30:8 (TPT) every day for a month: "Empty out of my heart everything that is false—every lie, and every crooked thing." Then, take some time each evening to journal about the things that come up. Don't be surprised if you become far more self-aware during this time. Your part is to partner with the Holy Spirit in prayer for your heart, and once things start being revealed to you, you take authority over them, capture the thoughts, repent, forgive, etc.

As you pray this prayer, your sensitivity to the Holy Spirit will increase, and your spirit will probably start to notice negative thought patterns, beliefs, or even hidden sin you might not be aware of. As God empties those things out of your heart, give Him thanks for opening your eyes up to what you couldn't see before. You were blind but now you see! Then, read Chapter 6 on meditation to learn how to fill in the gaps.

Notes

1 Andrew Wommack, *You Are as Plain as Dirt: What Type of Soil is Your Heart?* (Woodland Park, CO: Andrew Wommack Ministries, Incorporated, 2023).
2 *Ibid.*
3 C.S. Lewis, *Letters to Malcolm: Chiefly on Prayer*, (Boston, MA: Mariner Books, 2002).

CHAPTER 6

MEDITATING TO PLANT

Remember, Jeremiah 1:10 says, "Look, I have put my words in your mouth! Today I appoint you to stand up against nations and kingdoms. Some you must uproot and tear down, destroy and overthrow. Others you must build up and plant."

Now, picture this:

You're sitting in your favorite chair with a cozy blanket draped over your legs. A candle flickers against the still-dark morning. Your Bible sits on your lap, and a cup of hot coffee rests in your hands. This is the position you find yourself in at the start of every day, and you would not miss it for the world.

As you go through the scriptures, you think about how wonderful they sound. Familiar verses are like old friends, and stories jump out to you in new ways. However, in the back of your mind, you can't shake the lingering belief that some of the truth is not for you.

There are too many inconsistencies:

- "Ask, and it will be given to you" (Matthew 7:7 ESV). *I ask You every day, God.*
- "Give, and you will receive" (Luke 6:38). *I tithe, but my bank account still struggles.*
- "Peace I leave with you; my peace I give you" (John 14:27 NIV). *Anxiety still prowls like a lion.*

What do we do when we don't believe the Bible? When we acknowledge the truth in our head but can't get it to land in our hearts?

As Christians, we don't talk about this disconnect enough. Faith and hope are not automatic. They require careful cultivation and brutal honesty with oneself and God. When we doubt and feel distant from God, the key is to draw nearer. Meditation is how we bridge the gap between our heads and our hearts.

Thomas Watson said, "Without meditation, the truths of God will not stay with us."

I Believe, but Help My Unbelief

Anna was 25 years old when she became pregnant for the first time. She and her husband, Dean, had been married just shy of three years and were ecstatic. Throughout the first month of her pregnancy, they dreamt up the baby's name and personality, traversed the aisles of Target to look at baby clothes, and pictured themselves holding a newborn at Thanksgiving and Christmas gatherings.

Then one evening, Anna started to bleed. A lot. They rushed to the emergency room and discovered she was most likely having a miscarriage. There was nothing to do but go home and wait. Anna and Dean prayed constantly and rallied their friends to do the same. They read every psalm in the book and declared scriptures on healing. The bleeding did not stop. Ten days later, they went to the doctor for another ultrasound. There was no baby.

Fast-forward six months, and two pink lines appeared again. The same feelings rose to the surface—joy, relief, hope, gratitude—but others did as well: fear, sadness, hesitation, and anxiety. Would this baby be okay? It took more strength for Anna and Dean to imagine themselves as parents than it did in the first pregnancy. Anna struggled to picture her stomach growing and, later, her baby.

The places where we need to heal are the places where we have been hurt before. When we have not seen God's goodness in a certain area of our lives, discrepancies between the Bible and our beliefs form. The fear of disappointment makes it harder to hope.

The "what if I don't heal" starts to sound louder than the "but what if I do?"

This is a difficult position to be in. Sometimes, we want to have faith but can't come to that place by ourselves. Mark 9:23-24 (NKJV) tells the story of a father who knew this tension well. An evil spirit possessed his son from birth, and he asked Jesus to help him.

Jesus said to him, "If you can believe, all things are possible to him who believes."

Immediately the father of the child cried out and said with tears, "Lord, I believe; help my unbelief!"

How often do we find ourselves in this place? We cannot force hope upon ourselves, but we can pray, "Lord, I'm ready to start hoping" or "I want to trust You again," and meditate on scriptures that feed those desires. In fact, scripture repeatedly reveals that meditation is the key to prospering in every area of life:

Oh, the joys of those who do not follow the advice of the wicked, or stand around with sinners, or join in with mockers. But they delight in the law of the Lord, meditating on it day and night. They are like trees planted along the riverbank, bearing fruit each season. Their leaves never wither, and they prosper in all they do (Psalm 1:1-3).

Healing from Disappointment

Let's bring it back to Anna and Dean's story. When they got pregnant after loss, it was really hard for them to see themselves in the promise of becoming parents. At first, every symptom triggered images of losing the baby again. Experiencing the joy that would come with their baby's birth felt nearly impossible. This is natural after a loss of any kind. Proverbs 13:12 tells us, "Hope deferred makes the heart sick, but a dream fulfilled is a tree of life." God is not angry at us when we are heartsick; He is eager and ready to heal us. Psalm 34:18 reminds us that, "The Lord is close to the brokenhearted; he rescues those whose spirits are crushed."

Our challenge is to let God heal us.

The remedy to Anna and Dean's hopelessness was not to try harder to be hopeful. Many people try to work hard at having faith, which is impossible! They slide right back into religion, not relationship.

It's like Paul said in Galatians 3:3, "How foolish can you be? After starting your new lives in the spirit, why are you now trying to become perfect by your own human effort?" When we try to force ourselves to have faith, hope, and trust, we place the burden back on ourselves. Instead, meditation allows us to give our burdens back to God. Through meditating on who God is and what He has done, we focus less on our deficiencies and more on God's faithfulness and unfailing love.

I love how Romans 3:27-28 puts this in *The Message*: "What we've learned is this: God does not respond to what we do; we respond to what God does. We've finally figured it out. Our lives get in step with God and all others by letting him set the pace, not by proudly or anxiously trying to run the parade."

Anna and Dean's solution was to rely on the grace of God. They did not force themselves to believe in their own strength. Instead, they prayed prayers like, "God, I don't have what it takes to trust You right now. Empower me to see the situation how You see it." Then, they mined scripture to find verses that applied to their prayers, and they meditated on them day and night:

> *When they walk through the Valley of Weeping, it will become a place of refreshing springs. The autumn rains will clothe it with blessings* (Psalm 84:6-7).
>
> *And it is impossible to please God without faith. Anyone who wants to come to him must believe that God exists and that he rewards those who sincerely seek him* (Hebrews 11:6).

Meditating to Plant

> *You crown the year with a bountiful harvest; even the hard pathways overflow with abundance* (Psalm 65:11).

> *I wait quietly before God, for my victory comes from him. ... Let all that I am wait quietly before God, for my hope is in him* (Psalm 62:1,5).

Anna and Dean eventually found the strength to trust God with their story. With each passing week, they received more boldness to pray big prayers and get their hopes up again. To their surprise, they found out that near strangers who did not even know they were pregnant were praying for their baby's health! Instead of PTSD, doctor's appointments were filled with peace and redemption as they saw their baby bounce around on an ultrasound. Eventually, they gave birth to a healthy baby boy.

Andrew Wommack calls this process graduating from faith to trust. As we go through the healing process with God, there comes a point when we have to let go of our idea of how or when something should happen. We must trade our personal idea of what the outcome should be for God's ultimate plan. You can lean on God when you do not have enough faith to carry you through. Ask God to help you have faith when you feel like you can't have faith any longer. Ask Him to help you trust Him, even when you feel like He let you down in the past. You will be healed, see profound redemption, and grow your faith exponentially. Like Dean and Anna, you will experience the power and presence of God in your hardest moments. In fact, God doesn't just promise peace, He promises perfect peace.

Every issue in life grows out of our hearts, and meditating on the Word of God is how you plant the right seeds. When you meditate on great things, great things will grow and come to pass in your life. Meditation is the process of turning head knowledge into heart knowledge. Psalm 119:11 describes it as hiding the Word of God in our hearts. Meditating on scripture plants the truth so deeply inside of us that it becomes our second nature, and the Word of God becomes a part of our identity.

We can talk all day long about what we know, but we will reproduce what we believe. It is a fact of life. Biologically, we pass our DNA to our children. God made us to "be fruitful and multiply" (Genesis 1:28), and we multiply who we are. Our mission is to "make disciples of all the nations," and those disciples will reflect the faith we model (Matthew 28:19). We cannot impart something we do not have. So, if we want to live lives that produce a thirty-, sixty-, and one hundredfold harvest, it starts with meditating on scripture so that it becomes revelation not just information.

When you meditate on scripture during the day, it becomes part of your subconscious thought process in the night. Psalm 16:7 says, "I will bless the Lord who guides me; even at night my heart instructs me." What you think about during the day affects your dreams, subconscious thoughts, and body while you sleep.

In the last chapter, you learned how to reveal these subconscious thought patterns and negative beliefs through prayer. As the Holy Spirit exposed strongholds, you uprooted any thoughts and lies that opposed the Word of God. Now, you are ready to plant the seeds that will allow you to heal and prosper in every season. So, what exactly is meditation?

Meditation: What It Is (and What It Is Not)

Biblical meditation looks a lot different than the world's version of meditation. Believers from other religions, like Buddhism, meditate to empty themselves. In samatha meditation, for example, they focus on their breathing and try to let go of any thoughts that come to mind. On the contrary, Christians meditate to fill themselves with the Word of God. Rather than detaching, Christian meditation involves deeply connecting to the truth of who God is and who you are. It is not vain repetition but a focused and intentional way of saying scripture with your heart.

Whether you know it or not, you are meditating most of the time. The majority of your thought life is a meditative process. Meditation involves thinking about an issue, goal, or situation until it gets into your heart and affects you subconsciously. Have you ever been so troubled by a problem that it kept you up at night? If so, you know how to meditate!

We can meditate on positive and negative things, and research shows that, unfortunately, the latter is more common. According to The U.S. National Science Foundation, we rarely have new thoughts. The majority of people think 90 percent of the same thoughts as yesterday, and 80 percent of those thoughts are negative.[1] That is why the last chapter about uprooting through prayer is so important. After you eliminate the negative images, unhealthy beliefs, and destructive memories, it is time to fill in the gaps with scripture. Joshua 1:8 says, "Study this Book of Instruction continually. Meditate on it day and night so you will be sure to obey everything written in it. Only then will you prosper and succeed in all you do."

Did you catch that? Meditating on scripture is the key to prospering in every area of your life! This can serve as a spiritual check for you. If you are not prospering in every area of your life, it could be because you are meditating on the wrong things. For example, someone may be prospering in their relationships and career but their finances are struggling. In this instance, that person is probably recycling a negative thought process about money rather than a biblical one. Your health and outward prosperity are intimately linked to your soul's state.

Check this out—3 John 1:2 (NKJV) says, "Beloved, I pray that you may prosper in all things and be in health, just as your soul prospers." Many times, we leave our meditations unchecked. For example, we will do a devotional for 15 or 30 minutes in the morning and have an awesome time with the Lord. But as soon as we get in the car to go to work, we start beating ourselves up and dwelling on our pasts. Then, something bad happens at the office, and there goes our day! When we get home from work, we wonder why we are so burned out and exhausted. If we want to prosper in all we do, we must get beyond our daily Bible study and meditate on the Word of God day and night.

How to Meditate

Martin Luther, theologian and father of the Protestant Reformation, meditated daily. He referred to his practice as a "garland of four strands" meditation method. First, Luther thought about what a scripture was instructing. Then, he offered thanksgiving, confession, and prayer in light of the scripture. He credited meditation as one of the chief things that transformed his heart and said, "There is however a difference between meditating and thinking. To meditate means to think persistently, deeply and diligently. Properly speaking, it means to chew over something in the heart."[2]

Meditation may sound super lofty or spiritual, but it doesn't have to be. Just like prayer, meditation is most powerful when it is simple and personal. As a teenager, the only scripture I memorized was Philippians 4:13, "I can do everything through Christ, who gives me strength." Whenever I got into a tough spot, I remembered that verse, and it gave me the endurance to keep going. When I was 18, I went on the mission field full time as a translator across Latin America. Four others and I drove three vehicles of equipment across Mexico, Central America, and Brazil to host crusades with over ten thousand people. It was exhilarating, but it was also intimidating. Every time we had to cross the border, I was responsible for communicating with the guards since I was the only one who spoke Spanish. I had to explain that we weren't selling items or sneaking in contraband, and it took hours of conversation and paperwork. When I felt weak, Philippians 4:13 circled through my mind and gave me strength. I knew that God would make a way for us to continue to do our work.

If you find scriptures that speak to the areas where you want to grow or heal, meditation will not feel like empty repetition. Recall what you want to uproot, tear down, overthrow, and destroy. Ruminate on verses that directly combat the lies and negative beliefs you discovered through prayer. As you read your Bible, ask the Holy Spirit to highlight certain verses.

As you meditate on the Word of God in the middle of tough situations, it becomes more personal. Scripture becomes embedded into your memories. Then, when more difficult moments arise, your gut reaction will be to recite scripture rather than to spiral into fear and worry. That is why Psalm 119:11 describes meditation as hiding the Word of God in our hearts: "I have hidden your word in my heart, that I might not sin against you."

We can have things other than the Word of God hiding in our hearts, too, like subconscious thought patterns and habits that cause us to fall short. Often, these are unintentional and second nature. For example, nobody eats a cupcake with the goal of making their health worse. Yet, when not regulated, sugar and unhealthy eating habits become addictive over time. Reaching for the bag of chips or mindlessly eating Oreos in front of the television becomes automatic.

Like food, we metabolize our thoughts. We put food in our mouths and chew, but the process does not stop there. (If it did, we would die!) Rather, our bodies metabolize the nutrients from the food to provide strength and function in our bodies. (Or, depending on what we eat, it makes us lethargic and unhealthy.) Similarly, we internalize our thoughts, and they affect our actions. If you want to change how you act, change how you think first. Remember, God gave us neuroplasticity—the power to physically transform our brains by changing our thoughts.

God showed me the power of this firsthand by healing a broken relationship I had with a good friend. He stole $5,000 from me, and, after his thievery, acted like it was nothing! It's amazing how quickly that situation became the only thing I remembered about him in the midst of years of great experiences together. This one negative instance in our friendship quickly took up more mental real estate than the countless good times we had shared. It's so easy for one offense or betrayal to override a multitude of good memories. I was just so angry and shocked that my friend could do something like that.

It's safe to say that the meditation of my heart was not pleasing to God! Forgiving him took me a while, but I knew that forgiveness was not a feeling—it was a choice. Still, the bad taste in my mouth remained whenever I thought about him.

One day, I was reading the Bible, and Philippians 4:8 popped off the page, "Fix your thoughts on what is true, and honorable, and right, and pure, and lovely, and admirable. Think about things that are excellent and worthy of praise." Paul penned that scripture in prison, yet he was able to remain positive. In a much different way, I felt imprisoned by negative and anxious thoughts whenever I thought about this friend. If Paul could put positive meditation into practice in such dire circumstances, I knew God could help me do the same in my situation. So, I felt a tug in my heart to remember that scripture and meditate on it throughout the week.

Many times, we understand Philippians 4:8 in a general sense and simply try to maintain cheery thoughts. That's not a bad practice by any means, but God showed me the power of applying that verse to people and painful memories. A few days later, I started thinking about the betrayal. The Holy Spirit reminded me of Philippians 4:8 and prompted me to apply it to this specific situation and person. At first, I questioned if it was even God. I knew I had to forgive him, but did that really mean that I had to think good things about him too?

The answer was yes. Little did I know that the Holy Spirit was giving me a key to unlocking the healing process in this instance and future situations as well.

So, instead of letting my emotions take over, I chose to recall the good memories we had shared. It was definitely a battle to take my thoughts captive when they naturally wanted to scream, "Remember what he did!" However, as time passed, focusing on his true, honorable, and lovely qualities became easier. After just ten minutes, the presence of God in the room was incredibly strong. That's when I knew that the supernatural peace of God was removing pain and making me whole. And that wasn't even the craziest part.

Later that week, I went to a restaurant, and somebody paid my bill. The waiter pointed out my benefactor, and it was the very same friend sitting at the table with his dad! In disbelief, I walked over and thanked him. With his eyes watering, he wrapped me in a hug. I found out that his dad was super sick, and they were visiting town to go to a specific hospital. So I prayed for his dad, and he was miraculously

Meditating to Plant

healed! That's the power of meditating on the Word of God. He will bring the right people into your life at the right time and restore situations that you thought were irreparably broken.

Forgiveness and healing are separate processes, and they occur on different timelines. You can forgive someone while still needing to heal from the pain they caused you. In other words, you can still experience triggering memories, negative thoughts, and a lack of trust after you forgive someone. That's why Philippians 4:8 is so powerful in the healing process. Your brain is accustomed to taking the easiest route. It's like taking a road trip through the mountains. Your destination may be 50 miles from your current location, yet you have to drive 200 miles because that's the only paved route through the rocky terrain.

Similarly, your brain tends to think along paved routes by retracing your most frequent thought processes. Philippians 4:8 is how you carve a new road with thought patterns that are true, honorable, right, pure, lovely, admirable, excellent, and worthy of praise. It's how you build a bridge that goes from forgiveness to healing. The key is to retrace the right roads until you truly believe the positive thoughts you tell yourself.

You can tell if you believe something based on your reaction to pressure and difficult circumstances. Threats to your belief system reveal your true beliefs. For example, many Christians would say that they believe in God's healing and protection. Yet, the COVID-19 pandemic put those beliefs to the test. Many Christians closed churches, isolated, and were consumed by fear.

Here's another illustration. Many Christians say that they believe in God's provision. They trust that when they give, they will receive. Yet, the minute they lose their jobs or economists project a recession, they stop tithing and hoard their finances. Faith requires believing the Word of God despite what the external circumstances look like. It involves hoping for healing even when tests come back unfavorable, and the disease appears to be getting worse.

So, what do you do when your reactions don't line up with what you thought you believed?

First, recognize that even if you agree with a scripture, it does not mean you believe it yet. Acknowledge that it was head knowledge, not heart knowledge, and meditate on scripture that speaks to the truth. You plant a seed every time you hide a new scripture in your heart. As you put scripture inside of you, you compress the truth deep within your subconscious. So, when life puts on the pressure and you get squeezed, your instinct will be to praise and trust God amid hard circumstances.

Visualize Yourself in the Scripture

You know that the Word of God is becoming a part of you when you can start picturing yourself in scripture. A member of my church calls this "remembering your future." Imagine that you are your future self—the person experiencing the very hopes and dreams your present self is praying for. It's not enough to read scripture and think, "That's a great word." We must see ourselves in God's promises as well.

Then, the next step is to use your imagination until you actually feel as though the promise is coming to pass in your life. This is what we call a sanctified imagination, and it's how we operationalize our faith. A good way to consider this is to consider how fear, the opposite of faith, works. When we fear, we experience ourselves and our loved ones going through the worst possible scenario. Not only do we imagine it, but we also feel it and exhibit symptoms as though the scenarios are actually happening. Our brains do not know the difference between reality and imagination. That's why our hearts race, our bodies sweat, and we have panic attacks when we experience fear. It's all from a fearful imagination that may never even happen.

Thankfully, meditation has the power to renew our imagination. You can experience genuine gratitude, joy, and praise when you meditate on God's promises. If you really believe in healing, you won't imagine the world coming to an end in the middle of a global pandemic. Instead, you'll see something like angels surrounding you in the midst of death and disease. You can confidently know that a scripture has made its way from your head to your heart when you can start to feel what it is like to be inside that promise. Many people don't want to go to this place because they are afraid that it won't happen. So, they stay surface level, content to agree but never to believe and claim scripture as their own. They never dare to hope because they fear being disappointed again.

Hebrews 11:1 says that faith is the substance of things hoped for. So, faith without hope is worthless. On the other hand, if we have hope, faith will materialize what we hope for. That is why it is so important to make scripture personal and see yourself inside of it.

Shalom Shalom

Isaiah 26:3 (ESV) tells us, "You keep him in perfect peace whose mind is stayed on you, because he trusts in you."

When you continually fix your thoughts on God rather than yourself, other people, or your problems, the result is perfect peace. This kind of peace goes deeper than feelings of tranquility and implies more than the absence of fighting. In Hebrew, the phrase for "perfect peace" is *shalom shalom*. Old Testament writers used the same word twice to emphasize the intensity of this heavenly peace. In fact, the root word of *shalom shalom*, means "to make something whole."[3] *Shalom shalom* is wholeness and healing with God, yourself, and others. It brings anything that is in disorder into perfect order. Throughout the Old Testament, the phrase is used to describe completeness, safety, soundness, health, prosperity, contentment, friendship with people and God, and welfare (Strong's H7965).

Shalom shalom was the state of the Garden of Eden, and it will be the state of the New Jerusalem when God restores all of creation. You can access *shalom shalom* today, and it starts in your mind.

As Isaiah 26:3 says, your experience of perfect peace depends on your thoughts. When they are stayed, or fixed, on God, it means that you are in a state of trust where you can cast all of your cares on

Him. According to *Strong's Concordance*, the word *stayed* comes from the root "to prop" and embodies the idea of leaning on something (Strong's H5564). The same word is often translated as *sustain*. The implications of this are huge. Whatever your thoughts rest on determines whether you are in a state of peace or anxiousness. Meditating on the Word of God has the power to sustain you and maintain you in perfect peace. However, to be kept in *shalom*, your thoughts must stay fixed on the truth day and night. Though you will inevitably have time where you fall, your mind will get stronger as you practice. Your default will be to prop your thoughts on God, even when resting.

When you keep your thoughts fixed on God, your actions will follow. As Romans 12:2 says, when you change the way you think, "you will learn to know God's will for you, which is good and pleasing and perfect." God's will for your life positions you in *shalom shalom*. This is a state of internal harmony among you, yourself, and God. In this harmonious state, anxiety, depression, and demonic thoughts must flee. It is also a state of external harmony in your relationships, community, and world. *Shalom* is the type of peace that redeems and restores you back to God's original intent for man in the Garden of Eden before the enemy entered and there was a curse over your work and reproduction. It frees you to fulfill God's original Genesis 1:28 blessing for humanity: "Be fruitful and multiply. Fill the earth and govern it. Reign over the fish in the sea, the birds in the sky, and all the animals that scurry along the ground." *Shalom shalom* allows you to experience the joy of God's presence in every detail of your day. It also enables you to share the glory of co-creating and partnering with God to restore others to the same perfect peace.

Chapter Summary

- You cannot force hope or healing, but you can pray, "Lord, I'm ready to start believing" or "I'm ready to hope for my healing" and meditate on scriptures that feed those desires.

Meditating to Plant

- Every issue in life grows out of your heart, and meditating on the Word of God is how you plant the right seeds. When you meditate on great things, great things will grow and come to pass in your life.
- As you meditate on the Word of God in the middle of tough situations, scripture becomes embedded into your memories. Then, when more difficult moments arise, your gut reaction will be to declare scripture, remain in peace, and produce life rather than to spiral into fear and worry.
- When you meditate, envision yourself inside of the scripture. Envision what it would be like to receive the promises it describes.
- Meditation leads to:
  - Prospering in every area of life (Joshua 1:8)
  - Resisting sin (Psalm 119:11)
  - Perfect peace (Isaiah 26:3)
  - Ultimately, healing! (Proverbs 4:22)

Activate: Get Specific

Meditation is an essential ingredient for wholehearted healing. The key is to get really specific about the unhealthy beliefs and lies that the Holy Spirit revealed in prayer. Write them down, then find scripture to replace the lies with truth.

Here are some examples from people in our congregation at Vida Church:

Lie: I'm fearful, and I'll always be afraid.

> Scripture: *"I sought the Lord, and he answered me and delivered me from all my fears"* (Psalm 34:4 ESV).

Lie: It is difficult to have success.

> Scripture: *"Commit your work to the Lord, and your plans will be established"* (Proverbs 16:3 ESV).

Lie: Nothing turns out right for me. I can't get things done.

> Scripture: *"Fear not, for I am with you; be not dismayed, for I am your God; I will strengthen you, I will help you, I will uphold you with my righteous right hand"* (Isaiah 41:10 ESV).

Lie: I am crazy.

> Scripture: *"'For who has understood the mind of the Lord so as to instruct him?' But we have the mind of Christ"* (1 Corinthians 2:16 ESV).

Lie: I have no talent. I'm not really good at anything.

> Scripture: *"For we are his workmanship, created in Christ Jesus for good works, which God prepared beforehand, that we should walk in them"* (Ephesians 2:10 ESV).

Lie: I can't be healed.

> Scripture: *"He himself bore our sins in his body on the tree, that we might die to sin and live to righteousness. By his wounds you have been healed"* (1 Peter 2:24 ESV).
>
> *Behold, I will bring to it health and healing, and I will heal them and reveal to them abundance of prosperity and security* (Jeremiah 33:6 ESV).

Lie: I'll never overcome this addiction. I need it to feel good.

> Scripture: *And I find that the strength of Christ's explosive power infuses me to conquer every difficulty"* (Philippians 4:13 TPT).

These are powerful examples, now the key is for you to see yourself in that scripture and start feeling it as your new reality. Through this meditation, you're bringing about the Kingdom of Heaven into your life. This is how you make the realities of heaven yours.

Notes

1 Prakhar Verma, "Destroy Negativity From Your Mind with This Simple Exercise, November 27, 2017," https://medium.com/the-mission/a-practical-hack-to-combat-negative-thoughts-in-2-minutes-or-less-cc3d1bddb3af.
2 John W. Kleinig. "The Kindled Heart: Luther on Meditation," *Lutheran Theological Journal*, Vol. 20, 1986, 2.
3 Bible Study Tools, Shalam, https://www.biblestudytools.com/lexicons/hebrew/nas/shalam.html.

CHAPTER 7

DECLARING TO BUILD

In the beginning, God spoke. He said, "Let there be light," and there was light.

> *And God saw that the light was good. Then he separated the light from the darkness. God called the light "day" and the darkness "night." And evening passed and morning came, marking the first day* (Genesis 1:4-5).

The story continues, and God proceeds to create everything that has life simply by speaking it into existence. With a word, the vast oceans and spacious sky spread across the earth. Towering trees and delicious fruit bushes burst from the ground. The sun, moon, and stars took their place in the cosmos. Fish leapt in the sea, birds soared in the air, and animals scurried on the ground. Finally, God formed humans to steward it all. The apostle John called Jesus "the Word," and confirmed that, "The Word gave life to everything that was created, and his life brought life to everyone" (John 1:4).

We are made in God's image and have the Word living inside of us. So, the words we say have power. It is so amazing to me that the first example of what God did with His words was creation, not communication. We need to act more like God and have the same goal to create with the intentional, faith-filled words coming out of our mouths. I believe most humans use their words for communicating and hardly ever to intentionally create. I'd dare to say that most people are destroying or creating a dark future when they speak the hopeless, dark beliefs lurking within their hearts.

Declaring to Build

Now that you have meditated on the truth and planted it deep in your heart, it is time to declare it out loud. From Genesis 1 to present day, declaration is the essence of all creation. Our words compose the building blocks of our reality.

To put it simply, "declaring to build" is the practice of speaking out loud the truth from the Word of God that I believe in my heart and expecting something powerful to happen. It is having the belief and seeing in my imagination the effect of those words.

Second Corinthians 4:13 (NASB) says, "I believed, therefore I spoke." This tells me that just speaking doesn't mean much until my words are backed up by my belief in what I'm saying.

Proverbs 18:21 confirms that our words can build or destroy. It says, "The tongue can bring death or life; those who love to talk will reap the consequences." Oddly enough, the home furnishings store IKEA ran an experiment at schools in the United Arab Emirates that illustrated the truth of this verse. The goal was to show the destructive effects of bullying. IKEA's team members set up two identical IKEA plants in the school, and for 30 days, they invited students to compliment one plant and bully the other. Each plant got the same amount of sunlight and water. After 30 days, the encouraged plant was healthy and thriving. The insulted plant was noticeably wilted and droopy.[1] Our words are like energy packets, and their contents have tangible effects on our environment.

The childhood chant, "Sticks and stones may break my bones, but words may never hurt me," is a lie! Our words make a profound impact on the world, and other people's words make a profound impact on us. When we declare the Word of God, we actively give it more authority than our feelings, our circumstances, or what other people say.

Words Reveal Your Heart

Not all of the words you speak come directly from your heart. As people, we tend to say a lot of things we don't believe, this includes good and bad things. We say things like, "I'm blessed and highly favored" (while not believing one ounce of it) or things like, "I wish

I had never married you!" (not true but a poor choice of words in an emotionally charged moment). However, a lot of the words we speak repeatedly do give us a very good idea of what we believe. Our common reactions to stressful situations also give us clues into the contents of our hearts.

So, if you want a glimpse into your heart, pay attention to the words you speak. Jesus compared the words we speak to fruit. He said, "A tree is identified by its fruit. If a tree is good, its fruit will be good. If a tree is bad, its fruit will be bad" (Matthew 12:33). This is why we have to be so intentional to uproot, destroy, overthrow, and tear down the unbiblical beliefs. Now that our heart is less junky and we have planted the seeds of God's Word through meditation, we can produce good fruit.

Jesus continued, "For whatever is in your heart determines what you say. A good person produces good things from the treasury of a good heart, and an evil person produces evil things from the treasury of an evil heart" (Matthew 12:34-35).

Now, does this mean that we never lie, say things we don't mean, or make a joke? Absolutely not! Some people get really religious with this and freak out at statements that are not meant to be taken seriously. They become the "word police" and believe me, they're not fun to be around. These people don't realize that they're only responsible for the words they speak, not everyone else's words. Declaring the truth sets you free—it should not make you feel like you have to walk on eggshells or tiptoe around every word you say.

Sometimes, we believe more in curses than we do in blessings. I remember the story of a pastor who put this theory to the test. One Sunday morning, he got in front of his congregation and pulled out an ancient-looking book.

He said, "Good morning, church! Today, I want to read a bit from this crazy book of witchcraft spells I found so you can see how ridiculous this really is." Immediately, the room became tangibly uncomfortable. People began to squirm in their seats, and many were eyeing the exit; some stood up and discreetly started walking out. In the tension, the pastor paused. Then, he said, "I'm not actually holding a witchcraft book, nor would I read from it, but I wanted you to notice how much more you believe in curses than in blessings just based on your obvious reactions right now. You certainly don't get this excited when I read to you from the Book of Life or pray a blessing over you each week!"

When I heard this story, I thought it was hilarious but also eye-opening. When we speak the Word of God, do we actually believe it holds truth and power that can transform our lives? This is a crucial component of declaration. The words you declare will only have power when you believe them in your heart.

Cognitive Dissonance

When your mouth agrees with your heart, it is powerful. In fact, Romans 10:9-10 confirms that it is the very source of our salvation. It says, "If you openly declare that Jesus is Lord and believe in your heart that God raised him from the dead, you will be saved. For it is by believing in your heart that you are made right with God, and it is by openly declaring your faith that you are saved." Believing in our hearts and declaring with our mouths is how everything in the Kingdom comes to pass.

But somewhere along the line, people got it twisted and forgot the belief portion of the equation. Many Christians think that anything they say has power. They think it's like the Miranda Rights: "Everything you say can and will be used against you in a court of law!"

In fact, there is a danger when people go around declaring things they don't believe. It creates cognitive dissonance, which is the phenomenon of holding two conflicting beliefs or attitudes. In other words, it is an internal hypocrisy between your head and your heart.

You may have seen cognitive dissonance operate on a macro level in some churches and organizations. Some pastors and churches preach a message that God's grace saves us, not what we do. They say all the right things, yet their operations run counterculture to their message. There is a culture of fear, and as people get a closer view, they get hurt. What they feel when they walk into the room is very different than what's being preached. So, people start to question the validity of church and the Christian faith at large. When moral failures get exposed in Christian leaders and pastors, this same painful pattern repeats. In short, cognitive dissonance can happen in a congregation when leaders don't practice what they preach.

On an individual level, cognitive dissonance occurs when we declare something without believing it in our heart of hearts. For example, we can declare scriptures like Isaiah 53:5 (NIV), "And by his wounds we are healed," but still feel there must be a reason we are not qualified to receive healing. Or we declare 2 Corinthians 8:9, "So that by his poverty he could make you rich," while we still feel unworthy or even uncomfortable uttering the word *rich*.

I want to be clear about this, we can *know* things in our head that we don't *believe* in our hearts. We *know* things in our conscious mind, which is the left side of our brains, but we believe things in our hearts, which is really the right side of our brains where our subconscious is. It's in the right side of our brain where our "identity" is stored. This is why we can say what we know (left brain knowledge), but we create from what we believe (right brain beliefs). That's what differentiates between something we heard or learned and simply agree with, and something that is truly ours, part of us, a core belief or something we live by. I wanted to lay this out because it will help us understand cognitive dissonance better and the dangers of this internal hypocrisy.

With that being said, people go around saying or declaring things they know are right but do not necessarily believe. Many times, they don't even know that they don't believe them, which is what leads many into frustration, confusion, and new wrong beliefs in efforts to explain why some biblical promise hasn't worked for them the way it has for others.

We have to also understand that our heart (subconscious right brain) will win every time it fights against our mind (conscious left brain) regarding any idea. The left side of the brain runs at 5 Hertz and the right side runs at 6 Hertz. Identity wins every time, good or bad. I can learn a new biblical principle that tells me I'm a child of God, but if my heart continues to believe I'm not enough and I'm an orphan, it will drown the new revelation and kill it. Then I will continue to act and live like an orphan because my heart belief is still that of an orphan's. This explains why many times we fight this duality of what we know is true from God's Word and what we continue to live out.

One of the biggest known cognitive dissonances among many Christians is the question of whether we are sinners or righteous. Many pride themselves on calling themselves sinners saved by grace and fewer believe they're actually the righteousness of God in Christ Jesus. Those who believe to be sinners saved by grace struggle more with sin because at their core, they still believe they're sinners. And sinners are gonna sin sin sin sin. Those who truly believe they're now righteous by grace stop sinning because that is not who they are anymore. Identity dictates their behavior, not the other way around. Learning to live and operate from the heart, the place where our identity lives, is the way of living by grace. Living by grace means we are empowered by God. The opposite, however, is living out of knowledge (knowledge puffs up, 1 Corinthians 8:1), which hard work. In this life, we try to behave in order to determine our identities. It is a works-based system.

So we must learn to live from the heart!

We need to align our mouth with our heart, and we will see those things manifest in our lives. Most people speak what they know and see nothing created. Speaking what we know and expecting power to manifest is like shooting blanks. They're empty of power. On the other hand, speaking what we believe, what is ours, what comes from who we are, is full of power and will create and manifest God's Word.

This internal hypocrisy that many live with is very harmful. It is like having a house divided against itself right inside of us. We know and say something, but we don't always believe it. It sounds good. It's truth. But it's not ours yet because there are bigger, deeply seeded, opposing beliefs fighting it. These are the wrong beliefs we need to uproot, destroy, overthrow, and demolish so that we can plant and build the Word of God in our hearts and produce a hundredfold!

Salvation comes because you believe it in your heart and say it with your mouth. Healing comes because you believe God can and wants to heal you, and then you declare that aloud. Otherwise, you will become frustrated that healing is not happening and think, "I have to declare it more! I have to declare it louder!" This compulsion can be painfully prevalent when you know God's promises but don't experience them.

You can only reproduce what's in your heart. For example, Jesus tells us that the greatest command is to love God and love others (Matthew 22:37-38). However, what do you do when you realize that you don't actually love the people in your office or church? Do you pretend and try to convince yourself that you love them? No! If you do, you will experience cognitive dissonance with love because your head says you should love, but your heart knows you don't. If you want to reproduce the fruit of the Spirit, you must invite God into that space. Confess your true feelings and ask Him to help you love others like He does. Then, meditate on and declare biblical truths that have to do with love. That's a prayer He will answer every time!

Regarding healing, your declaration may need to be, "I'm ready to believe for my healing," not, "I'm healed, I'm healed, *I'm healed!*" When my leg was recovering from the dirt bike accident, I didn't go around and profess my healing as if I was ignoring the screws attaching metal bars to my femur and tibia. Instead, I said, "God's power is at work inside me, and today will be better than yesterday." Faith doesn't deny the problem; it takes away its power to become bigger than God in your life.

If you don't fully believe a biblical truth, don't try to convince yourself out of feelings of inadequacy or shame. This will only make you feel distant from God or like a hypocrite. Instead, ask God questions like:

- What in my heart is so strongly opposing this truth?
- Why can't I believe this promise is for me?
- What toxic belief, negative image, or destructive memory is opposing Your Word in me?

Declaring to Build

If you want to have faith, God will lead you to a faith that will do immeasurably more than you can ask or imagine (Ephesians 3:20). However, if you ignore the process of combating cognitive dissonance, you will only create more internal conflicts and delay the manifestation of God's revealed Word in your life. The Holy Spirit is amazing and will lead you into all truth (John 16:13). So, whenever the Holy Spirit makes you aware of your cognitive dissonance, be encouraged! Now you know exactly what to pray to uproot and have a blueprint of what type of scriptures to meditate on.

Faith That Moves Mountains

One afternoon, Jesus was hungry and in search of a snack. Mark 11:13-14 says,

> *He noticed a fig tree in full leaf a little way off, so he went over to see if he could find any figs. But there were only leaves because it was too early in the season for fruit. When Jesus saw that there were not any figs on the tree despite its luscious leaves, He declared, "May no one ever eat your fruit again!"*

Jesus was more than just hangry here. He didn't curse the tree because it didn't have fruit; He cursed the tree because it didn't have fruit while it was acting like it did. This was a metaphor for the Pharisees and religious leaders who followed the law and upheld strict standards but were not bearing the fruit of God: love, joy, peace, patience, kindness, goodness, faithfulness, gentleness, and self-control.

When Jesus and the disciples passed by the fig tree the following day, it was dead.

> *Then Jesus said to the disciples, "Have faith in God. I tell you the truth, you can say to this mountain, 'May you be lifted up and thrown into the sea,' and it will happen. But you must*

> *really believe it will happen and have no doubt in your heart. I tell you, you can pray for anything, and if you believe that you've received it, it will be yours"* (Mark 11:22-24).

At that time, "mountain" was a popular figure of speech for any colossal problem. When you declare God's Word without doubt, He will do what appears to be impossible in your life. Jesus urged the disciples to believe in their hearts, not just to profess that they believed. He did not want them to be religious people who looked the part on the outside but were missing core parts of their faith on the inside. In other words, Jesus does not want you to be like the cursed fig tree! When you ask for something in faith, you need to believe that you have received it before you see the results of your prayer with your physical eyes.

In the same teaching, Jesus discusses forgiveness with the disciples. He tells the disciples, "But when you are praying, first forgive anyone you are holding a grudge against, so that your Father in heaven will forgive your sins, too" (Mark 11:25). God cares more about the condition of your heart than He cares about you doing big things for Him. It's like God is saying, "I care more about your character than all the amazing things you're going to do with that money I give you." You can't have a large capacity in the Kingdom of Heaven without having strong, godly character.

So, faith-filled words have the power to create or destroy. They are how you do the "build up" portion of Jeremiah 1:10. The question now is, what are you building?

Just like God created the world with the words He spoke, you, made in His likeness and image, can also create the world you live and experience with the power of your words—specifically, the words you deeply believe.

Speaking Life Over Yourself

Through prayer, you've identified any mindsets and strongholds contrary to God's Word. In meditation, you've replaced those

Declaring to Build

negative thoughts by planting the seeds of scripture. The Word has been working inside of you, and now it's time to declare those truths aloud.

Let's say that you are sick and have struggled with the following lie: "My condition is a unique case, so God won't heal me," or "I've had this sickness for way too long. It's a part of me now, so healing won't work for me."

For scriptures, you meditated on Isaiah 53:5 and Matthew 4:23-34. Now, your declaration involves reading those scriptures and a truthful statement aloud.

Scriptures

But he was pierced for our rebellion, crushed for our sins. He was beaten so we could be whole. He was whipped so we could be healed (Isaiah 53:5).

Jesus traveled throughout the region of Galilee, teaching in the synagogues and announcing the Good News about the Kingdom. And he healed every kind of disease and illness (Matthew 4:23).

Statement

I receive healing, and I hold on to the Word of God that tells me I am healed. I take my thoughts captive moment by moment. Lord, reveal anything in my soul preventing me from receiving all You have for me, including perfect health. I am worthy of wholeness. I do not need the attention that sickness brings; sickness is not part of my identity. I am seen, heard, loved, and appreciated without sickness.

When the lie, "Nothing turns out right for me," crawls into your head, you'll have the ammo to destroy it.

After your declaration statement, do a heart check. How true did it feel when you made your personalized biblical declaration? Could you imagine yourself healed? Were you able to feel any emotions associated with what you were saying? Or did the words you were saying feel fake? Answering these questions is how you can check what your beliefs truly are. Then, you'll know whether or not to pray, "Yes! This truth is mine. I can fully see and feel it." Or, "I'm starting to believe this is mine!" Or, "I believe, but help my unbelief."

Remember, the purity of your belief matters more than the words you say. One belief-packed word has more power than a litany of lies. Jesus illustrated this when He and His disciples were out at sea in the middle of a terrible storm. The disciples were terrified, yet all Jesus said was, "Quiet! Be still!" Immediately, it was calm (Mark 4:39 NIV). Jesus gives you the same power and authority. However, that power can only flow through your internal belief system. Jesus did not have any negative images, unhealthy beliefs, or destructive memories that hindered that flow. That's right! That is a huge difference between Jesus and you. His belief system was fully aligned with God's Word; therefore, everything He spoke came out without any unbelief filters, no opposing beliefs, no cognitive dissonance, no doubt, no internal fight. And you can observe the powerful results of His ministry on the earth. He gave you permission to do the same and more! He gave you His name and authority. You just need to do the heart work to be fully aligned with God's Spirit and Word. How exciting!

So, the more you destroy ungodly strongholds and build biblical ones, the more your heart will truly believe the Word of God. Then, as you declare those good things, you will eat the good fruit of the promises you speak, like Proverbs 18:21 promises!

Intercession Through Declaration

We established earlier on that prayer is not begging God, nor is it trying to convince Him to do something He's against. We've also established that we are agents of heaven with the authority to bring about God's purposes and promises to earth. We are the agents of reconciling people to the Father through Jesus. God needs our prayers, and He needs us to do our part so He can do His. Like I always say, we do the natural, and He does the supernatural. This all happens in partnership with God; so when we have hidden His Word in our hearts and are now speaking power-filled words, creating and manifesting heaven like Jesus did, our intercession takes on a whole other level.

The more you know the Word of God, the more authority you carry because you know what is needed in every situation. You must learn how to release and operate in the opposite spirit of what is attacking or negatively influencing a situation.

This is where declaration gets really exciting. We know that God wants to bring His Kingdom to earth, and scripture gives us plenty of insight into Kingdom assets like peace, justice, and joy. So, when we declare peace in a chaotic situation, God moves. When we declare justice amid oppression, God moves. When we declare joy in the midst of hopelessness, God moves.

It only takes a small amount of faith to move the mountains in your world—the places of pain, suffering, and brokenness. Again, Matthew 17:20 says, "I tell you the truth, if you had faith even as small as a mustard seed, you could say to this mountain, 'Move from here to there,' and it would move. Nothing would be impossible."

At the end of this chapter's summary, I have provided examples of what to declare. The next chapter will break down the biblical prayer I've been telling you about so you can pray it over your heart daily. You will see tremendous breakthrough and healing at a rapid rate when you understand and start praying this prayer!

Chapter Summary

- God first used words to create, second to communicate. Your words can be faith-filled power packets you use to create your reality.
- Declaring the Word of God is how you take your authority when interceding and build yourself and others up. It is also how you advance the Kingdom of God when you are praying.

- Belief is an essential component of power-filled declarations. When you don't believe the words you say, you create cognitive dissonance, a form of internal hypocrisy that causes you to be divided against yourself instead of in agreement. So, the goal is to align your mouth with your heart.
- When you declare God's Word without doubt, He will do what appears impossible in your life.
- When you ask for something in faith, you need to believe that you have received it before you see the results of your prayer with your eyes.

Activate: Declarations

So, how do you know what to declare? Like meditation, it is best to declare scriptures that align with the areas where you want to grow or where you need breakthrough. What lies do you need to replace with truth? Where do you want to see a breakthrough? What reminders do you need to cling to throughout your day?

I like to use the fruit of the Spirit as a guidepost to help me evaluate the areas where I need to grow. For example, if I'm dealing with depression or I continually find myself sad and feeling weak, I look at the fruit of the Spirit and realize I'm lacking joy, which is the opposite spirit. I identify what's been robbing my joy, and then I'm ready to declare scriptures of joy. As I'm declaring these scriptures, I need to be brutally honest with myself and assess how much I believe what I'm saying. Let's say I only believe it 50 percent—that's okay and very healthy to recognize so that I don't feel guilt and condemnation or end up creating cognitive dissonance trying to tell myself I fully believe it. Next, I need to meditate on these scriptures day after day, seeing myself in the picture, feeling the scriptures becoming mine more and more each day. I then track that percentage as it increases day after day. This could take a month of daily meditation because you have to remember, you're bringing down strongholds you've built up your whole life.

Here are some examples of declarations based on the fruit of the Spirit. Be sure to modify them and make them personal:

Love

God loves me so much that Jesus gave His life for me. He gladly meets every need. He's intensely interested in every detail of my life, and He equips me with everything I need to serve Him well. He delights in who I am and rejoices over me with singing.

Joy

Every day is a gift, and I choose to open each one with joy and gratitude. Happiness depends on circumstances, but joy comes from the fruit of the Holy Spirit inside me, regardless of external circumstances. I choose joy. God creates desires in me so that He can have the joy of fulfilling them. He wants to give me the desires of my heart. As I trust Him, He will not withhold any good thing from me.

Peace

As I trust in God, He keeps me in perfect peace. He is perfect, and His way for me is perfect, grounded in His great love for me. I can always be at peace knowing God wants to bless me.

Patience

I wait patiently for God in His love to give me what I need when I need it. I can relax completely in His love and care, knowing He's leading me toward a glorious future. As I cease striving and trust God, He works mightily in my life.

Kindness

Those who have been harsh with me were probably treated that way themselves at some point. I choose to forgive them and sow seeds of kindness and compassion.

Goodness

The Lord is my Good Shepherd. I lack no good thing, and I can count on God to shower His goodness and mercy on every area of my life.

Trust

I can trust in my Lord with all my heart, knowing that He gladly and lovingly meets all my needs and brings good things into my life. He also heals all my wounds and diseases. I can bring all my troubles to Him, for He cares for me, understands my pain, and delights in answering my prayers.

Faithfulness

God is faithful to fulfill His promises to me. My future dreams and current assignment are from God. God will empower me to be faithful as He is faithful. I can work diligently, knowing that the one who is faithful with little can be entrusted with much.

Humility

I accept my human limitations and my needs. I do what is 100 percent under my control and trust God to take care of the tasks, people, and events I cannot get to or control. I cease striving and choose to let God be God. I put my hope in God's unfailing love, not in what people think of me.

Self-Control

I can do all things in Christ Jesus, who gives me strength. He has given me the power to tell myself what to do and to obey the voice of the Holy Spirit even when it is uncomfortable or when my flesh is fighting against me. I surrender to God and live by His principles. As I delight in God, He gives me the desires of my heart.

Note

1   Global News, "IKEA conducts a bullying experiment on plants—the results are shocking," https://globalnews.ca/news/4217594/bully-a-plant-ikea.

CHAPTER 8

A BIBLICAL PRAYER FOR WHOLEHEARTED HEALING

Now that you have made it this far together, you have the puzzle pieces you need to heal any area of your life and achieve breakthrough wherever it's needed. Jesus gave us access to His finished work on the cross. The more freedom, wholeness, victory, and prosperity you experience, the more Jesus receives the rewards of what He paid for you to have. He came that you might have life and have it more abundantly (John 10:10).

You now have knowledge about prayer, meditation, and declaration, as well as simple ways to use these tools in ways you didn't know before. Now, the next step is to put the pieces together. That's the part I'm helping you with. Prayer, meditation, and declaration is something you've probably known for a long time, but how and where to use them to achieve wholeness, healing, and breakthroughs from lifelong cycles is something most people don't know. It is time to put this revelation into action so that you can actually experience lasting transformation! We have covered the what, but this chapter is all about the how.

Let's make it practical and get down to the daily application. It is, however, extremely important that you understand all this before just taking the biblical prayer and reciting it every morning and turning it into religion, which would then make it powerless.

God showed me the biblical prayer as a way to pray according to the promises outlined in His Word. As you pray this prayer, the goal is to partner with the Holy Spirit to intentionally address the missing, broken, and unknown pieces keeping you from wholehearted healing. Like we discussed in Chapter 5, prayer is not about saying the right words in the right order, but about believing what you're saying.

I encourage you to pray this daily as you go through the healing process. Doing so has revolutionized my life, my wife's life, and countless lives in our congregation. It's a prayer from your heart and for your heart. Each line derives from scripture, so as you read it aloud each day, you will be meditating on and declaring truth.

Here's a testimony from a woman at my church named Jean, who suffered from migraines and chronic sickness:

> The biblical prayer is great for asking the Holy Spirit to pinpoint false beliefs that produce pain in our lives and bodies. Since I started to pray it, I no longer get migraines. I used to get sick all the time, especially around big jobs and events like my birthday. Thanks to the heart work, I am much healthier now! God has set me free to a new level that is high above my former beliefs. I no longer use sickness as a shield to hide me away when I don't think I'm good enough for something.

At the end of the day, the question is, "What inside of me is directly opposing the truth of the Word of God from working in me?" Jean realized she was inviting sickness into her life because she felt inadequate. She wanted an excuse that would somehow allow her to forgo her responsibilities or explain why she viewed herself as underqualified. Through this prayer, God revealed how loved and truly valuable she was, which helped combat the sickness. Similarly, the biblical prayer will help you remove any self-defeating lies that keep you from walking in the fullness of life and health.

This prayer is not meant to replace your daily devotions, and it should take seven minutes max, depending on what you're working on. It is a robust way to combine everything you have learned about healing in this book. When we pray this prayer, we are praying to uproot, tear down, destroy, and overthrow the negative images, unhealthy belief systems, and lies that oppose the Word of God. We are meditating to plant and hide the Word of God in our hearts. Finally, we declare God's Word to build and bring about the realities of heaven and God's promises.

So, let's break it down section by section so you can understand what you're about to pray.

Invite the Holy Spirit

"Holy Spirit, I ask You…"

The Holy Spirit is the person of the Trinity who is with us on earth to lead us into all truth and freedom. John 14:26-17 says that He is our advocate, comforter, encourager, and counselor. John 8:32 confirms that through Him, "You will know the truth, and the truth will set you free." The more you go through this prayer, the greater levels of freedom you will experience. Jesus set you free. He opened the prison doors and removed the shackles of everything that bound you. Now, it's your job to follow Him out of the cell. Many Christians stay in their prison cells even though Jesus unlocked and opened the door already. In this prayer, you start that process by asking God to reveal the areas holding you captive.

In Psalm 139:23, King David prayed, "Search me, O God, and know my heart." That is exactly what you'll be asking for in this prayer. The Holy Spirit is the one who searches your heart, so you can't do the heart work without Him. You can't heal yourself, and you can't try to fix all your issues at once. As Jesus said, "Apart from me you can do nothing" (John 15:5). You might think, "Well, I can do some things." That's true. We can all do some things. However, you can't do the supernatural or anything of eternal value alone. If you have been waiting for healing and have not experienced it yet, it is time to let the Holy Spirit take over.

The Holy Spirit leads the healing process and knows the correct order of operations. He deals with the issues that are harming you the most. If someone who is smoking and drinking turns to the Lord, religion wants to modify that person's behavior right away. However, the Holy Spirit's agenda could be completely different. The Holy Spirit might want to address the root of the issue first and the symptoms of smoking and drinking last. He knows that person's heart, so He knows where the problems and addictions started.

Ask the Holy Spirit to Find the Known *and* the Unknown Issues

We all have blind spots. There are belief systems hidden in our subconscious that we don't know we don't know. Even though we don't recognize them, they profoundly affect our lives because they're always in the background calling the shots. We need the power and light of the Holy Spirit to illuminate them. Like David, we need to pray: "How can I know all the sins lurking in my heart? Cleanse me from these hidden faults" (Psalm 19:12). Letting the Holy Spirit lead your healing journey requires surrendering your understanding (Proverbs 3:5-6). Don't come to Him holding a diagnosis and a prescription. Instead, ask Him to highlight the unknown areas where you need healing. This is the difference between a relationship and a religion. A religion says, "Tell me the right things to say and do so that I can control the outcome." A relationship says, "I want to be with You, and I trust You to walk me through life when I'm in the dark."

You can't plan for or pre-process God. Instead, you experience Him. When you declare this biblical prayer, inviting the Holy Spirit looks like asking questions such as:

- What do You want to talk about today?
- What do You want to restore today?
- What do You want me to believe for today?
- What are we going to do today together, as daughter/son and Father?

Ask the Holy Spirit to Find Three Specific Things

"...to find all negative images, unhealthy beliefs, destructive memories, and all physical issues related to _____ in my body/life."

Fill in the blank with the area where you need healing. This could be a physical issue, like high blood pressure, diabetes, allergies, leg pain, or stress. Or it could be something less tangible, like anger, addiction, fear, financial problems, or lust. When you do this, you are really saying, "Find the root issues, Holy Spirit." We can trace most of our health issues to our thought life, whether physical, emotional, relational, or financial health. (Remember, 98 percent of health issues are related to stress!) So, as we discussed early on in the book, our healing depends on us taking our thoughts captive and renewing our minds to the Word of God. However, we must be able to identify those negative images, unhealthy beliefs, and destructive memories first. The Holy Spirit will help you do just that in this prayer.

Negative images are when your perception of normalcy goes against God's intent and design. For example, the mental pictures you have about the following could put a roadblock in your healing if they oppose biblical truth:

- Money = evil
- Marriage = hard
- Healing = impossible
- Men = abusive
- Women = weak
- Parenthood = stressful
- Church and serving God = boring
- Sex = dirty
- God = angry

Those are seven examples of the negative images many people have. They're not biblical views about those subjects and negative images can certainly affect those aspects of your life and greatly obstruct God's will for you. Each one of those words to the right come with an image and many times that's all there is to it. No story, no context, just an image that impacted you from a real-life situation or even a fictional one like a movie or something you saw in a magazine or online.

At some point, you unintentionally conformed to the world and adopted its images of what God had created perfect. Then you started associating everything in that category with the same negative images. That is why so many Christians are not in church. They had a negative experience of church, so they kept a negative image of church, and it's hard for them to try it again. Money is another excellent example. Many people in the body of Christ have a negative, Scrooge-like image of money. They adopted a belief that it is bad for Christians to care about money, so they associate it with greed, loneliness, and self-centeredness. So, every time a good opportunity for a financial breakthrough shows up, their subconscious sabotages it. You have negative images of many things, but that doesn't mean those images represent the truth. God wants to heal them so that you can see how He sees. God will give you new images to replace the old negative ones.

Unhealthy belief systems are ideas surrounding a certain topic that oppose biblical truth. Another name for unhealthy belief systems is strongholds. To review, we build strongholds one thought at a time by gathering evidence that supports those beliefs. For example, the enemy whispers the lie that you don't belong. Then, you let anything that resembles rejection confirm that lie until you are convinced it's true. And even if you have acceptance staring you in the face, you run the high risk of rejecting and sabotaging it because your stronghold has a need to be right. Ultimately, strongholds are mental defenses that prevent us from knowing truth and experiencing abundant life with God.

In this process, you "take every thought captive to obey Christ," as 2 Corinthians 10:5 (ESV) instructs. Many unhealthy beliefs are robbing people from living the abundant life. "All men are evil," "My family will always be broke," "Good things don't last in my life,"

"Everyone betrays me," "I'll never find a godly spouse," "God is mad at me and He's punishing me," etc. This is how the enemy steals, kills, and destroys (John 10:10).

A woman named Christy from my church has a powerful testimony about the impact this part of the prayer had on her life:

> God healed me from the fear of man—I used to be such a people pleaser! He told me that I was never alone and immediately took away the fear of abandonment, which I didn't even know I had. In addition, I am completely off one of my medications, and the dosage for two others has been lowered.

Christy lived with a hidden stronghold of abandonment her whole life until God revealed it to her. As she tore down the stronghold, physical issues also started to heal. Our physical healing is often linked to a root issue we wouldn't know anything about without the power of the Holy Spirit.

Destructive memories are memories of the past that tear down your image of yourself, God, or others. Even though they may have happened long ago, they still sting and hold you back from experiencing the fullness of life. If you are a parent, you may have heard of the Law of Firsts. Essentially, it means that the first time children hear about something is very important because that voice will become the authority on that subject. So, if your children hear about sex for the first time from a friend at school, that friend is going to be the authority that your kids measure every other fact and opinion against (even if that friend does not know anything).

This is also why our early experiences in church can be so detrimental. Let's say you grew up in a legalistic, fire-and-brimstone church that depicted an angry picture of God. At first, it will probably be harder for you to accept God as a gracious and loving Father. We store memories about every topic under the sun from the first time we heard about them. So, pay attention to the memories the Holy Spirit brings to the surface during your prayers. They are key indicators of the root issues.

A Biblical Prayer for Wholehearted Healing

Destructive memories can be conscious or subconscious. Just like we have muscle memory, we have cellular memory, too. Our cells have memories that go all the way back to before we were born! My wife has a powerful testimony about this. When she was in the womb, her mother was going to abort her. Even though she didn't know about this until she was an adult, it affected her self-worth and sense of belonging. There were memories of rejection from when she was going to be aborted in her cells. (God healed her, but more on that later!)

In addition, our parents and grandparents pass down generational curses even on a cellular level. When I say curses, I am more referring to the ungodly practices and unbiblical views we've inherited from them. Things that we now need to fight for ourselves to align to God's way. Generational curses can be in the form of addictions, divorce, toxic behaviors, pagan traditions, ungodly world views, even toxic reactions, and more. These are not blessings that were passed down but instead curses. Things we caught even if they weren't taught.

When I refer to generational curses passed down on a cellular level, I would recommend reading Dr. Caroline Leaf's *Switch on Your Brain* where she details her extensive research on how our DNA carries things passed down to us like potential cancer, addictions, criminal behaviors, etc. I don't believe generational curses as many Christians would think of them. I don't think there are curses passed down to you that you have no power over or that there are curses you are a victim to or that you need to address everything your parents did in their lives in order to break those curses. I believe we are responsible to address the areas in our own lives that are absent of abundance and prosperity, and that will sometimes be connected to something you inherited from your parents or grandparents. If the Holy Spirit reveals that, then you address it. But I'm not a believer in going on wild, endless witch hunts. The Holy Spirit leads us to all truth.

On the other hand, we don't want to be like the stubborn Christian who is suffering terribly and keeps declaring he's a new creation, blessed and highly favored and therefore there's no generational curse in his life. Maybe there is.

Traumatic memories or PTSD are another category of destructive memories that affect our lives. If you remember, God healed me from this after I had the accident. I couldn't even get in a car or drive until the Holy Spirit healed those memories from the accident.

So, in this prayer, we are saying, "Holy Spirit, find all inherited, cellular, conversational, and traumatic memories that are holding us back from abundant life, prosperity, and wholeness." The next step after the Holy Spirit reveals these memories is to invite Him to heal them.

Co-Labor with God to Take the Territory of Your Heart

"I ask You to open them and heal them…"

Once you are aware of the negative images, unhealthy belief systems, and destructive memories that are hiding in your heart, your healing depends on kicking them out for good. This is the part of the prayer where you work with God to uproot, destroy, overthrow, and tear down any unwanted giants and inhabitants in the land of your heart. The good news is that God goes before you and behind you to help destroy your enemies. When you ask Him to open up and heal what's hurting you, you invite Him to fight on your behalf.

Remember, God helped the Israelites overcome their enemies in the Promised Land. So, He will help you overcome any problem, illness, or addiction that's harming you. As Deuteronomy 11:23 (NIV) says, "Then the Lord will drive out all these nations before you, and you will dispossess nations larger and stronger than you." Once your heart is open and healed, there is room for it to be filled with more of God's goodness.

Ask God to Fill Us with His Light, Love, and Life

"…by filling me with Your light that drives out all darkness and exposes the hidden things; with Your love that casts

out all fear; with Your life which makes all things new and restores all things; and with Your precious blood that redeems all things in my timeline."

Light

As John 1:4-5 says, "The Word gave life to everything that was created, and his life brought light to everyone. The light shines in the darkness, and the darkness can never extinguish it." When we ask God to fill us with His light, we ask Him to expose any darkness inside of us. His light exposes our blind spots, sins, and hidden motives so that we can repent and become whole. His light allows us to see what we couldn't see before, the unknown issues. When I pray for His light to fill me up, I imagine Him walking into my heart and turning on the light. Everything exposed before Him, I still feel His mercy, not His judgment. Now the hidden things can't stay there.

Love

When the love of God fills our lives, fear has to leave. First John 4:18 (NIV) says, "There is no fear in love. But perfect love drives out fear, because fear has to do with punishment. The one who fears is not made perfect in love." During this part of the prayer, I pause to recognize God's deep love for me. I visualize His love filling up the images, memories, and toxic beliefs that have long been influenced by fear; and as I see His love pouring in, I see fear being washed away, making me feel safe and secure in Him.

God is love, and perfect love casts out fear. So, any destructive memories, unhealthy belief systems, or negative images rooted in fear go away and lose their power. In the absence of fear, faith is activated and no longer contaminated!

Life and His Precious Blood

John 14:6 tells us He is the way, the truth, and the life. Everything that has breath is alive because of God. He is the author of life. Scripture calls Him the beginning and the end. Romans 4:17 tells us that He is the God who brings the dead to life and calls the things that are not as though they were. You are alive not because all your organs are properly functioning but because His breath of life is still in you. The life of God is what will restore and make all things new in your life. When these known and unknown issues are identified, you are inviting the life of God to bring back life into the places where death has had influence. Remember that the opposite of the abundant life He has given you is barely surviving and death. When God heals these areas in you, He resurrects the parts of your body and soul you thought were long dead. God's will is for you to have abundant life now and in the life to come (John 10:10), which is why He sent Jesus!

Leviticus 17:11 explains, "For the life of the body is in its blood. I have given you the blood on the altar to purify you, making you right with the Lord. It is the blood, given in exchange for a life, that makes purification possible." When Jesus shed His blood on the cross, He made you right with God. His blood redeems all things and brings the dead things back to life, which is what you will be praying for in this section. It is the blood of Jesus that has the power to redeem your past and break off every chain. It is the blood of Jesus that qualifies you to receive all His promises. It is His blood that justifies you, and it is His blood that speaks a better word over you, a better word than the words that have been stealing, killing, and bringing destruction in various areas of your life. Areas that have also been bought with the precious blood of Jesus.

Believe for More Than You Can Imagine

> *"I also pray that You would do infinitely more than I have asked or even dared to imagine in this prayer. I trust You, I love You, and I thank You for Your power that is at work in me. In the Name of Jesus, amen."*

We serve the God of the impossible. When you pray this prayer, be confident that He wants to do and will do more than you ask or dare to imagine.

As Ephesians 3:20 says, "Now all glory to God, who is able, through his mighty power at work within us, to accomplish infinitely more than we might ask or think." So, let your imagination run wild. Don't be afraid to hope big. Dream about what it will be like to be a fully healed and entirely whole person. If you believe, God will blow your expectations out of the water!

In the biblical prayer, you will find a blank—fill in the blank with whatever you need healing from, whether it be high blood pressure, arthritis, cancer, digestive problems, infertility, abandonment issues, poverty, financial roller coasters, insomnia, hormone imbalance, depression, anxiety, fear, anger, church hurt, or anything that isn't abundant life. Pray this slowly and pause after each line, creating the space to listen to God and for you to be able to see what you're praying. Pay attention to the images and memories that come to your mind, especially the unusual ones. As I said in the beginning of the book, many people don't do the heart work because it is at this point that the painful things we have avoided start coming up. The problem is that they don't need to be avoided; they need to be healed so that they lose their sting in your life. So be brave, you're in good hands—the Holy Spirit's hands. When things come up, let's say a painful childhood memory, talk to God. Ask Him where He was when this happened. Maybe you need to forgive someone, and maybe God wants to rewrite and redeem a moment or situation for you. Have that conversation with your Heavenly Father. Then make sure you ask Him what He has to say or show you about that image, memory, or wrong beliefs that came up. He always has a word for you.

Laying Hands

Throughout the scriptures, Jesus laid hands on people when He blessed and healed them (Matthew 9:18; Mark 5:23; 6:5; 7:32; 8:22-25; Luke 13:13). The apostles laid hands on the sick and they were healed. They also laid hands on people to receive the baptism of the Holy Spirit. We see this many times throughout the New Testament as a way to heal the sick, cast out devils, and get people filled with the

RADICAL HEALING

Holy Spirit. Laying on hands is simple; when you pray and declare scripture over people, you place your hands on them and power flows. We are a conduit of God's power.

Just as power comes with our words, it also comes through our hands. The power of the Holy Spirit flows through our hands, just like electricity would if we were touching a bare wire. So here's a thought, why not lay hands on yourself when you're praying? I want to challenge you to lay hands on yourself strategically while you're praying the biblical prayer. There are key places in your body you can alternate through—your heart, your temples, your forehead, and the back of your head. I touch these places because one is where memories are stored. One is where the frontal lobe is. One is also where decisions happen and where trauma is kept. Just as I would lay my hand on someone's arm because that's where healing was needed, I will lay hands on the various places in my head where the root beliefs, memories, and negative images are stored, because that's the place where I need healing. Remember these are the centers everything is affected by. So lay hands on yourself, and take your prayer for yourself to the next level!

Let's dive into the prayer:

Holy Spirit, You know me better than I know myself, and I thank You for it. So I ask You to search my heart and find all the known and hidden negative images, unhealthy beliefs, destructive memories, and all physical issues related to _____ in my body/life. I ask You to open them and heal them by filling me with Your light that drives out all darkness and exposes the hidden things, with Your love that casts out all fear, with Your life which makes all things new and restores all things, and with Your precious blood that redeems all things in my timeline. I also pray that You would do infinitely more than I have asked or even dared to imagine in this prayer. I trust You. I love You, and I thank You for Your power that is at work in me. In the name of Jesus, amen.

CHAPTER 9

THE EVIDENCE OF A HEALED HEART

So, you've diligently been praying, meditating, and declaring. You've applied the biblical prayer from the last chapter to the areas where you expect healing. How, then, will you know when you are healed? What results do you have to look forward to at the end of this journey?

Whether the source of your pain is something physical, like a disease or the result of an injury, or emotional, like grief from the loss of a loved one or the betrayal of a friend, healing is always connected with *shalom*, the peace, presence, and power of God at work.

Through meditation, you have been putting Philippians 4:8 into practice: "Fix your thoughts on what is true, and honorable, and right, and pure, and lovely, and admirable." You can be confident that healing has occurred when you experience the next verse: "Then the God of peace will be with you."

Remember, biblical peace isn't just any kind of peace. It's wholehearted completeness, order in the midst of chaos, and a profound sense that things are as they ought to be. When you are healed, you will tangibly feel God's peace in the place where addiction, negative thoughts, and destructive memories used to have dominion in your life.

Another way to put it is that the "sting" is gone. First Corinthians 15:55 says, "O death, where is your victory? O death, where is your sting?" The places where death had a hold in your life have been healed with the life of Jesus. It's not like you get amnesia and suddenly forget everything that hurt you, but it loses its sting. It doesn't ruin your day anymore. It doesn't cause disease in your body anymore. It no longer has a sting of venom poisoning your heart or dictating your thoughts and the meditations of your heart.

Psalm 19:14 says, "May the words of my mouth and the meditation of my heart be pleasing to you, O Lord, my rock and my redeemer." This scripture becomes so easy when your heart is healed. Before your heart is whole, this verse can seem difficult to achieve and forceful, but when your heart is healed and the sting is gone it becomes effortless. This is the difference between works and performance and the grace of God empowering us. To watch your every wrong word and every wrong thought and to try and make it pleasing for the Lord without ever healing your heart is very much like trimming weeds. But when you address the source of those bitter thoughts and words and you partner with the Holy Spirit to heal at the root, the fruit changes, the words become sweeter, and the meditations effortlessly improve.

Biblical Prayer in Action

My wife's testimony of the biblical prayer was one of the first and most powerful ones we've experienced firsthand. One day, she woke up and felt off and abnormally tired. After a couple of months of this, she went to the doctor to get a full blood panel. Dr. Sarah helped her, and she got started on bioidentical hormones. About a year later, she was ready to get off all supplements. She asked God to heal her hormones and started praying the biblical prayer to see if she had any destructive memories or ungodly beliefs that could be blocking her healing from this hormone imbalance. She would do it day and night and day and night, and one day, a destructive picture came to her mind. The memories were of her at 6 months old. She was in a crib, crying, crying, crying; and nobody would pick her up. The Holy Spirit gave her that memory so she could heal it. Those memories were speaking "abandonment" to her body. The Holy Spirit showed her a new picture to focus on. She started visualizing Jesus going into her room, picking her up, and comforting her.

A few months later, my wife asked her mom about the memory, and her mom said, "Kara, that's when you got really, really sick, and you had to stay in the hospital. Your dad and I were divorced at the time, and I had to work. I was a single mom, and I had to work a lot." Her mom was devastated she had to leave her at the hospital alone all day long, and could only come see her at night.

Hearing this story for the first time clarified what the Holy Spirit had brought up after doing the biblical prayer morning and night and laying hands on herself. After renewing her mind to the new picture of Jesus picking her up, it took about four months, and her hormones were totally healed. She got off all bioidentical hormones. To this day, a few years later, my wife is healed and feeling great.

In this case, Kara didn't even know about these memories in her conscious mind, but they were certainly playing a part in her life. Once she partnered with the Holy Spirit to deal with this hormonal imbalance, the Holy Spirit led her to the root of the issue. In this case, it was a buried destructive memory that she wasn't even aware of. This was something only God would know. Once it was opened and addressed, this unknown issue lost its sting.

Many times we do know the memories and they're so painful we can't even think or talk about them. This is a sign that they're not healed. An open wound hurts, can't be touched, runs the risk of being infected, and takes up your attention until it heals. A scar is the evidence that something got hurt but is now healed. You can touch the scar and there's no pain, no risk of infection, and you hardly ever think about it. Ultimately, you know you have been healed when you remember the pain but the pain does not hurt you anymore.

I want to add that we don't always have to go through this process to receive healing. We always pray, take authority in Jesus' name, and command our body to be healed. It's when we don't see healing that we kick it up a notch! Jesus paid for it already, so I'm going to find out what's going on here. We have to remember that God cares about our physical healing just as much as He cares about our mind, heart, and soul healing.

Test Your Triggers

When you take your car to the mechanic because it's making a funny noise, what is the first thing you do after they make the repairs? You make sure the noise is gone! Similarly, we need to put our healing to the test. Let's say that you struggle with insomnia. As you go through the healing process, it's important to ask yourself questions like, "Am I sleeping better?" If you're dealing with anger, how have you been reacting to frustrating situations? If it's migraines, have you been experiencing relief from the headaches?

It seems basic, but many people pray for healing and never put themselves to the test to see if they were actually healed. One of the simplest ways to know if you are healed is to test your triggers. Take note of the situations, words, or people that had a tendency to inflame your pain in the past. Then, evaluate if they bring out the same feelings or if you notice a change in your reactions. I say "bring out" because no situation can "bring out" of you something that isn't "in" you already. If the bottle of ketchup is empty, it doesn't matter how hard you squeeze it. No ketchup is coming out. What comes out when you're squeezed gives you a very good idea of what and how much is still inside of you. Nobody can make you angry if anger isn't already present. People don't have anger issues; they have problems with patience. Many times, you don't have to go hunting for these triggers. God will bring them right to you.

Hurt from Spiritual Leaders

We had just gotten married, and I started leading worship in this thriving, amazing church. We loved our church and pastors, and I planned on staying there for the rest of my life. After almost ten years of serving under these pastors, we had an experience that led us to question our future and everything God had for us and our family. We came to the sad conclusion that we needed to leave our church in order for God's plan to be fulfilled in our lives. The vision and desires

The Evidence of a Healed Heart

God had given us were just not going to happen if we stayed there. This was one of the hardest decisions I had ever made.

I'm not a church hopper. I believe in the power of finding your church family and planting your family there, building something together, and changing generations with God's family. When we came to the point of having this difficult conversation, our leaders did not take it well. We craved a blessing and a good send-off from our spiritual parents, and we did not get it. It was a surprisingly hurtful event full of confusion, heartbreak, and pain. For a time, it was painful whenever I thought about them. Whenever we ran into them at events or conferences, we waved awkwardly, and I left feeling hurt all over again. But then, Kara and I started to learn about the importance of healing our hearts. As a matter of fact, it is one of the keys to longevity, especially in ministry!

Applying Philippians 4:8 to the situation, I meditated on how those pastors blessed my life. They gave me a space to use my gifts in the ministry and we learned so much about finances, marriage, parenting, and faith from them. There was so much good we received in those ten years that we served them. As I kept meditating on their true and honorable characteristics, taking captive the old negative, painful thoughts about them and about that situation, I felt God's presence; His *shalom* came over me and that sense of healing began happening inside of me at that very moment in my living room. I had only been doing this for 15 minutes but I knew I was healed from that hurt. I felt lighter. I felt a greater sense of peace when I thought about them, and I had a new sense of freedom.

It was within a week that I ran into them at a restaurant. My initial reaction was to walk the other way, but in a split second, the Holy Spirit reminded me, "No, you're good, remember?" I was like "Right! I'm good now."

This time, I felt a surge of love for them and headed their way to hug them. It felt so genuine. It wasn't faked or forced. I asked how they were doing, and the small talk quickly took me by surprise when they, in the middle of that restaurant, brought back the incident from years before. This time, the thing I expected least happened. They humbly apologized and took responsibility for their bad reactions at that time. True restoration happened that day, and our connection was restored! Now, they don't trigger me at all. Quite the opposite. Whenever I see or think about them, I rejoice in the healing power of God! My heart is healed from that situation! It has no hold on me. There's no more sting from that time. The enemy lost when I became whole! And the enemy will keep losing as you become whole in the broken areas of your life.

If you don't want to wait for a triggering situation to occur, you can test your thoughts. Imagine yourself running into the people who hurt you or being in similar positions that usually cause pain or frustration. What do you feel? What thoughts come to mind? When you are healed, it's not hard to think good things about what used to hurt you. You have passed the thought test if true, honorable, right, pure, lovely, and admirable things come to mind.

Examine the Fruit of the Spirit

Life with God often feels like a game of tug-of-war. One moment, you can feel connected and complete, and the next moment, you are struggling with temptations and debilitating thoughts. The apostle Paul describes this as a battle between our self-will and the Spirit. Galatians 5:17 (TPT) says, "The two incompatible and conflicting forces within you are your self-life of the flesh and the new creation life of the Spirit." As you've been meditating on and declaring the Word of God, you have been feeding your spirit side. As a result, you are on the fast track to freedom! You've torn down, uprooted, destroyed, and overthrown the old inhabitants of your land, and they don't have power over you anymore. The Holy Spirit has more room to flourish in your life.

Galatians 5:22-23 tells us exactly what we can expect: "The Holy Spirit produces this kind of fruit in our lives: love, joy, peace, patience, kindness, goodness, faithfulness, gentleness, and self-control." *The Passion Translation* refers to this fruit as "divine love in all its varied expressions" and that these qualities are "meant to be limitless."

The Evidence of a Healed Heart

So, a great way to evaluate where you are in the healing process is to examine the fruit of the Spirit in your life. If you were struggling with depression, are you experiencing more joy? If you were healing from a damaged relationship, is there more kindness in your heart toward that person and people in general?

Galatians 6:8 (TPT) lets us know this is a reasonable expectation, confirming that, "If you plant the good seeds of a Spirit-life, you will reap beautiful fruits that grow from the everlasting life of the Spirit." When you take the time to prepare the soil of your heart through prayer and plant good seeds through meditating on scripture, you can expect that good things will grow. Just like oranges grow from an orange tree, the fruit of the Spirit will naturally flow out of you through God's power. That's why we get so exhausted when we try to be joyful, patient, or loving in our own strength. God did not design us to force these virtues. They are meant to flow out of us when we're rooted in God. Only then can we experience and give others a limitless, eternal supply of the fruit of the Spirit.

This is where our core verse for this book comes full circle:

Today I appoint you to stand up against nations and kingdoms. Some you must uproot and tear down, destroy and overthrow. Others you must build up and plant (Jeremiah 1:10).

You have done the heart work—maybe it was about finances, or relationships, or diabetes, or high blood pressure, or depression—and now you feel healed, whole, and free in that area. You're starting to notice tangible changes, big and small breakthroughs, even things around you are changing (including some people), and you're even starting to attract healthier situations. It is so important that you notice them and celebrate them. You are responsible to be a good steward of your encounters with God and your victories and testimonies. Remember that every good thing comes from God (James 1:17), so thank God and give Him praise for it! You are now planting in good soil and building on the strong foundation. You can expect these areas of your life to keep growing and prospering.

Jeremiah 17:8 says you are:

> *Like trees planted along a riverbank, with roots that reach deep into the water. Such trees are not bothered by the heat or worried by long months of drought. Their leaves stay green, and they never stop producing fruit.*

A healed heart can remain strong in difficult times and remain fruitful in any circumstance. That is the future you can look forward to!

God has a big plan and purpose for your future. The more your heart is healed, the more you can freely fulfill your divine calling in the Kingdom of God.

It's important to end on this note. Healing isn't a one-time thing. Because we interact with broken people and live in a broken world, we will have to undergo this process time and time again. However, we move from glory to glory and become more whole with each issue we deal with. The journey to a healed heart is marked by continual transformation reflecting God's peace, presence, and power. When we live in this rhythm, we can experience a sense of completeness and order amid life's chaos.

My wife and I have continued to experience this over the years. The more we cultivate our heart and keep it free from bitterness and junk, the sweeter fruit our lives produce. It is this kind of personal testimony that confidently allows me to say to anyone who is willing to do the heart work, the best is yet to come!

Chapter Summary

- Peace, the *shalom* of God, is an indicator of healing. Order where there was chaos, ease where there was disease, and feeling the presence of God are indicators of a shift toward healing.
- When toxic beliefs, negative images, or traumatic memories are healed in you, it doesn't mean you get amnesia and all of a sudden

The Evidence of a Healed Heart

forget what happened but it loses its sting with you. It no longer causes you pain when you think of it. It loses the hold and weight and power it had over you, and the emotions it used to produce are gone or no longer negative. It's like it's been neutralized.
- Testing past triggers is crucial to assessing your healing progress. You can do this in person, or if that's dangerous or impossible, you can do it in your imagination. Your brain doesn't know the difference!
- Check your fruit! We harvest what we plant, so looking for evidence of the fruit of the Spirit or noticing what fruit of the Spirit is missing can steer you in the direction where you need attention. In addition, this reflection process can help you pinpoint areas where you still need to grow and heal.
- Jeremiah 17:8 portrays the healed heart as resilient and fruitful in every circumstance, rooted in God's eternal truth.
- Magnifying the victories creates an environment to get more of them. No matter how big or small the notices might be, when you magnify what God is doing, you'll get more of them.

Activate: Check the Progress and Magnify the Victories

Realizing your healing progress is simple, but you need to be intentional. You might think, "Well, if I'm healed, I'm healed, and I'll notice it when I notice it." Yes, but you could capitalize on your initial progress and create a snowball effect. What I mean by that is there's this principle I call "magnification principle." What you focus on, you get more of. Psalm 34:3, Psalm 69:30, and many more verses, including Mary in Luke, mention magnifying the Lord. God is already as big as He will ever be and will never shrink. But in our view, many times, we shrink Him in comparison to our problems. When we magnify Him, we keep Him as the most powerful and greatest force, making everything else pale in comparison to the greatness of our Heavenly Father. All that to show you how powerful it is when you magnify what the Lord is doing in you and how that sets you up to get more of it in all areas of your life. So be sure to magnify the small and the big advances you notice because you'll get more of them.

Journaling is a great practice to reflect on the day and evaluate how you responded to certain triggers. Brutal honesty with yourself is the only way to effectively make progress. There's no point in lying to yourself. You can do the biblical prayer in the morning, but if you have an anger episode at work, take your lunch break in your car and go pray. Specifically target patience. You can do this in as little as five minutes, and it's much cheaper than therapy or bail! As you read through your journal, you will see how your healing is progressing, and your heart will be worshipful! In turn, your faith will be strengthened because you can visibly see how God is empowering you to drive out the inhabitants of your promised land that have been splinters in your eyes and thorns on your side for way too long!

EPILOGUE

ONE OF MY SUPERNATURAL TESTIMONIES

There is a truer reality than the one you are used to. Colossians 3:3b (AMPC) tells us that our "[new, real] life is hidden with Christ in God." Gone is the life where self-improvement and comfort are the primary pursuits. With that being said, I want to commission you before we leave our time together. The purpose of becoming healed and whole is to be our most productive and efficient selves for the work that Ephesians 2:10 describes: "For we are God's masterpiece. He has created us anew in Christ Jesus, so we can do the good things he planned for us long ago."

We must see our healing process as something that will benefit others, not a self-centered pursuit. Our best life is not one of self-absorption. It's one of making disciples, pointing people to Jesus, and leading them to wholeness. Then, we will all work together in our calling as the body of Christ. As you continue becoming healed and whole, you give Jesus the reward for His suffering. Isaiah 53:5 says, "But he was pierced for our rebellion, crushed for our sins. He was beaten so that we could be whole. He was whipped so that we could be healed." When Jesus died for us, He took our sins, shame, sickness, and pain. Whenever someone benefits from His finished work on the cross, Jesus receives more of His reward. When we are healed, we can help others heal and give Jesus more glory!

RADICAL HEALING

I can only be a better husband, parent, friend, boss, employee, pastor, and leader to the measure that my heart is healed. Similarly, the best thing you can do for those you love and surround yourself with is continually cultivating your heart like a garden. Once you are healed, stay healthy. Maintain your heart and look for fruit. (For more on this, look for my next book on the fruit of the Spirit.)

I recently had to reexamine my heart when my church was in the process of looking for a bigger building. We had outgrown the location we had been renting for eight years. We looked and looked but found nothing. We prayed, had a building fund, and raised enough for a down payment. It came to a point where I had to ask myself the honest question, "Could I be the problem?" At this point, I had been teaching on the heart for many years, cultivating my heart to remain healthy, and producing good fruit. In a moment of desperation, I thought, *You know what, it can't hurt to check. I don't want to be the one holding back our church from all God has for us, so if something in me is blocking us from receiving this next building, let's deal with it!* I asked the Holy Spirit to correct any wrong images, memories, or beliefs related to finances, specifically finances in ministry. He showed me a couple of essential things. First, He reminded me that we were a Father and son duo. He wanted me to remember that His resources are my resources, so we always have enough and are building His house together. God wanted to settle these reminders in my heart before the next season of our family life and ministry.

At the time, I had a citrus tree in my backyard that had struggled to produce fruit for years. Where we live in Arizona is a prime climate for lemons, oranges, and grapefruits the size of your head, but our little tree didn't get the memo. It frustrated me, and I considered uprooting it for seven years. Yet, after this time with God, I walked outside and saw that two new branches had shot up out of nowhere. They didn't even look symmetrical with the rest of the tree and were twice its height. As I marveled at this, God said, "That's us. You and I are going higher together, unexpectedly and extravagantly."

A few months later, my family and I were about to leave for a beach vacation. We had already paid for the rental house, the kids had new swimsuits, and everything was ready to go. I was overdue for some rest and relaxation, but for the first time, I had no peace about going. Then, the owner of the rental house called to tell us that a few patio chairs had been destroyed in a small storm a few days prior. As a result, they offered us a full refund. I saw this as an out from God to cancel the trip, and we kicked it poolside for the week instead.

Monday, Tuesday, and Wednesday, I kept asking the Lord, "Why did we stay? I know You always deliver us from things, and I don't need to always know the answer. However, I sure would like to know if I missed it or why we could not go." Then, I received a phone call from a realtor I didn't know on Thursday morning. He asked me, "Are you interested in buying a church?"

That afternoon, my leaders and I went to view it. This church was only two miles from our current location, and the price was unbelievable. This realtor had a long list of churches to call, but he told me he decided to start calling from the bottom of the alphabetized list. So, Vida Church was one of the first contenders. That afternoon, our leaders agreed it was a fantastic opportunity. We submitted a letter of intent on Friday, and our offer was picked out of two other full price offers that had come before us, one of them being cash. We didn't have cash and needed owner financing, but they said yes to us despite our big requests.

If we had been on vacation, we would have missed the opportunity. I don't know how much of the cultivating of my heart a few months prior had to do with this open door, but I know it had an effect. I can't deny the fact that this miracle building came to us just months after I addressed my heart in this area, even when I thought my heart was all good in that area.

So, the lesson is this: keep doing the heart work. Remember, all issues of life flow from your heart, the bad ones and the good ones. So before trying new diets, new budgets, new church, new city, new methods for any issue, address your heart. Before thinking you're not qualified, you need to pray harder, fast longer, serve more, do more for God's promises to manifest, ask the Holy Spirit, "What unhealthy belief in me is keeping God's Word from being manifested in my life?" Apply the principles in this book again and again. Pray, meditate, and declare the Word of God. Your breakthrough is around the corner!

Reader, I pray that *Radical Healing* will serve as a tool that helps you become whole for the sake of your God-given calling. I pray that this simple revelation will lead you to experience breakthroughs with God. May you know Him as a Father who wants to do life with you. I pray that many will hear your testimonies of healing and that many more will taste the fruit that your life produces as a result. I pray for your heart's healing and a supernaturally quick journey. It doesn't have to be 40 years; some wounds can be healed in 21 days or 15 minutes.

I encourage you to pray your biblical prayer with understanding and teach others to do so as well. Thank you for sharing this journey with me.

Your Friend,
Ben Díaz

ABOUT BEN DÍAZ

Ben Díaz and his wife, Kara (author of *Living the Abundant Life*), are the founding pastors of Vida Church in Mesa, AZ. Ben began leading worship at the age of 15 at his parents' church in Mexico City, where he was born and resided until he became a missionary at 18. He then traveled across the US, Mexico, and Central and South America, leading worship, translating, and directing Miracle Crusades. Ben and Kara founded Heaven on Earth Homes, an orphanage in Kenya. They have five kids of their own and many adopted children in Africa.

In the Right Hands, This Book Will Change Lives!

Most of the people who need this message will not be looking for this book. To change their lives, you need to **put a copy of this book in their hands.**

Our ministry is constantly seeking methods to find the people who need this anointed message to change their lives. **Will you help us reach these people?**

Extend this ministry by sowing three, five, ten, or *even more* books today and change people's lives for the better! Your generosity will be part of catalyzing the Great Awakening that many have been prophesying and praying for.